What Are We Doing in Gym Today?

What Are We Doing in Gym Today?

NEW GAMES AND ACTIVITIES FOR THE ELEMENTARY PHYSICAL EDUCATION CLASS

Kenneth G. Tillman
and
Patricia Rizzo Toner

Illustrations by Patricia Rizzo Toner

Parker Publishing Company, Inc.
West Nyack, New York

Seventh Printing . . . . . April 1987

Library of Congress Cataloging in Publication Data

Tillman, Kenneth G.
  What are we doing in gym today?

  Includes index.
  1. Physical education for children. 2. Games.
I. Toner, Patricia Rizzo,   II. Title.
GV443.T565 1983   372.8'6   82-24606
ISBN 0-13-951822-3

Printed in the United States of America

I wish to dedicate this book to my parents, Mr. and Mrs. Darwin Tillman of Essex, Iowa. They provided me with encouragement from kindergarten through college and they have continued to provide unwavering support during the years that I have been a physical educator.

Kenneth G. Tillman

I wish to dedicate this book to my parents, Mr. and Mrs. Charles P. Rizzo of Clementon, New Jersey whose guidance and encouragement enabled me to further my education, and to my husband, Jess, who continually provides me with patience, loyalty and inspiration.

Patricia Rizzo Toner

How This Book Will Vitalize Your Physical Education Program

This book provides exciting and varied answers to the question, "What Are We Doing in Gym Today?" Every physical education teacher hears this question during the course of a school year. Sometimes the question is asked with eager anticipation and, at other times, with apprehension. This book contains over 300 games, activities, and variations that can be used as part of regularly scheduled physical education units; or they can be used to provide a variation in the type of activity that is provided. The emphasis is placed on creative activities and innovative ways of presenting the material.

This is not a physical education course of study. It is a compilation of different games and teaching approaches that have been used in physical education classes and found to add zest to the programs. There are activities and ideas that can be used in every unit that would be included in a K-8 physical education program.

The activities and games are unique and creative. If you are looking for new ideas to motivate students and make physical education a meaningful experience, the resources in each chapter are invaluable. You will also find that the activities are designed for coeducational use. Your coeducational program can incorporate the activities if you group your classes according to ability or schedule them on a heterogeneous basis. We have carefully considered the needs of coed classsses when selecting games and activities and providing suggestions for teaching procedures. You will discover that the materials provided in this book will significantly strengthen your coed program.

It is easy to get trapped into following the same procedure and teaching the same activities year after year. As a conscientious physical educator, you are constantly searching for new ideas. This book shares innovative teaching methods and creative games and activities that you can use in your programs. New activities and varied teaching techniques provide stimulation. This type of stimulation leads to increased creativity, which is very important to you. This book does more than present new games and activities; it provides a foundation from which creativity can evolve for you and your students.

This book is written for the elementary (K-8) level. Activities are provided for these age groups and they are designed to apply to a variety of teaching situations that you might have. Different student skill levels are considered through the scope of activities that are included in each chapter, and suggestions for modifying the activities and designing other games will permit you to make use of most of our material whether you teach the lower elementary grades or older students.

This book will give you access to varied games and activities that will increase the vitality of your curriculum. It can be the answer to your search for ideas that will make your classes more interesting and alive. We include information that will correlate with your physical education curricular materials and much of the material is appropriate to use as mini units to provide just the change that is needed to maintain student interest and keep enthusiasm for your program at a high level.

Our approach is to present a series of innovative and creative ideas that can be incorporated into your curriculum. A wide range of activities is included together with ideas to make your program challenging and enjoyable. You will discover that your students will become strenuously involved, mentally and physically, and they will have the opportunity to use and further develop their creative talents.

If you are looking for a wealth of ideas to use in your classes, our compilation of activities, not found in any other book, is for you. Several chapters are designed to provide breadth for your existing program. The activities in Chapter 1 will be ideal to expand the movement education component of your program. Chapter 2 provides new low-organization games that can be used by every teacher reading this book. The games are appropriate for use during physical education classes or during lunch and recess play time.

Chapter 3 encompasses lead-up games that can be used in a variety of ways. They can be used to teach your students the basics of sports such as soccer, field hockey, and basketball. They can be used just as effectively to provide an enjoyable way of modifying sports such as flag football, softball, and tennis.

Relay races are ideal for applying skills that are learned in physical education classes. They can also provide all kinds of mental and physical challenges for your students. Chapter 4 starts with relays that are very simple and can be completed quickly. Complex relays that will truly challenge your students follow. The novelty relays that complete the chapter will result in laughter and renewed student enthusiasm.

The final two chapters in this book tackle a major problem for most physical educators. How do you provide a stimulating physical education class with limited space or a large class? Over seventy different ideas in Chapters 5 and 6 will assist you in overcoming the space problem.

The games and activities in this book will strengthen student interest and vitalize your physical education program. The end result will be enthusiastic students who eagerly look forward to their physical education class.

Kenneth G. Tillman
Patricia Rizzo Toner

Acknowledgments

To Dee Tillman for typing the manuscript and for her helpful support as this book was written.

To Jess Toner for his valuable contributions and suggestions.

To the Health and Physical Education graduate students of Trenton State College, Trenton, New Jersey, who provided many of the ideas incorporated into this book.

To the students and Physical Education faculty of Council Rock Intermediate School, Holland, Pennsylvania, who tested many of the activities presented.

Contents

3   *Gee, This Is as Much Fun as Real Basketball*   87

116 Challenging Lead-Up Games and Activities

4   *Ready, Set, Go!*   **137**

38 New and Modified Relay Races

5   *Help...I Can't Breathe*   **163**

31 Ways to Utilize Limited Space

6   *I Hope to Get to Bat This Semester!*   **179**

Over 40 Ideal Games for Large Classes

What Are We Doing in Gym Today?

1

Where Do We Go from Here?

Adding Variety to Your
Physical Education Program
with 77 Movement Activities

Movement is the base of every physical education program. The success that your students will have with the activities contained in the other chapters in this book is determined by their movement foundation. It is for this reason that the first chapter is devoted to movement activities. A solid movement background is important for a student's future physical development. We feel that students must become familiar with how time, space, and force affect movement. They can then build on these concepts to develop the skills that are necessary for competence in sports and other physical activities.

We have included activities that you can use to vary your movement education program. This chapter sets the tone for the remaining chapters, which also emphasize the development of movement skills through new and modified games and activities.

Children must have the opportunity to learn how to use and control their bodies in a variety of ways. Movement activities in this chapter will make it possible for your students to experience different body positions and use their physical skills to explore their environment. This is done by using equipment such as hoops, ropes, and scooters, as well as by using body movements without the aid of equipment. We have designed the activities to fit within the concept of a child-centered approach. Each child is given the opportunity to experience the true joy of manipulating his or her body and to then apply this ability to all types of physical activity.

We make every attempt to provide sequential activities that encourage a child to progress from basic movement patterns to games of low organization, and then to more complex game activities found in the following chapters. We provide activities that will make it possible for your students to make full use of their physical potential.

A child's social success is often influenced by physical competence. Peer acceptance is frequently predicated on ability to perform physical skills. The movement approach to physical education, which is paramount throughout this book, develops your students' physical abilities at the level of their physiological readiness. This is extremely important to the psychological as well as the social development of each student.

Movement is an ungraded approach to physical education. Activities do not have to be designated for specific grade levels. We have found that children use the activities at their own level of readiness, and progression takes place as each child is challenged to utilize the concepts of time, space, and force, and apply them in the activities that are used. Children learn to manipulate objects and their own bodies in a progressively more complex manner. Basic movement patterns lead smoothly into tumbling, rhythms, lead-up games, games of low organization, and structured sports.

Movement activity is an educational vehicle to assist children in developing their physical skills in an enjoyable, positive atmosphere. They become aware of their physical capabilities and are able to use physical skills in adjusting to all aspects of their environment. You will be able to use the activities in this chapter to provide an enjoyable educational experience for your students.

MOTOR MOVEMENTS

BARTS (Beanbag Darts)

Object: To score the most points by hitting high scoring zones on the board with the beanbags or to be the first player to reach 21.

Equipment: Beanbags; dartboard made of plywood with dartboard zones set up on wall using tape lines or paint.

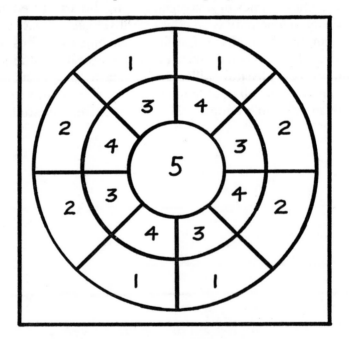

FIGURE 1-1. Diagram of dartboard for "Barts"

Description:

Players stand behind the foul line and alternately toss bean bags at the dartboard in an attempt to score points. Each player has three beanbags. The game can be played with a time limit where the person with the most points at the end of that time is the winner, or it can be played with the first to reach twenty-one being the winner. If a bag hits a line between two numbers, the lower point value is awarded.

SNOOPY

Object: To complete activities depicted by "Peanuts" characters.

Equipment: Posterboard depictions of "Peanuts" characters portraying different movement activities.

Description:

The "Peanuts" characters are placed at various places in the gymnasium with floor arrows leading to each character. The students move from character to character performing the movement activity depicted on each card.

When a student completes all the activities, give her a small cut-out of Snoopy.

Variation:

The same format can be used with ball skills, tumbling, hoops, and different kinds of physical education equipment.

RIVER FLOW

Object: To correctly complete the movement problems using water in cups, without allowing the water to spill.

Equipment: Water; paper cup for each student; towels; a mop.

Description: Movement challenges:

1. Walk around the room holding your cup of water, without spilling any.
2. Move in a funny way while controlling your cup.
3. Slide on your back while holding your cup in the air.
4. Hold your cup as high as you can.
5. See how many circles you can make in the air with your cup.
6. Invent a funny position without spilling your water.

7. In groups, or with partners, pass the cup back and forth.
8. Put your cup on the floor and cover it with your body. Pretend you are a flower opening its petals in the morning. Open away from the cup and then return to the closed position.

Variation:

Use small pieces of packing styrofoam instead of water.

SAM SELFISH AND SALLY SHARE

Object: To correctly perform the motor movements designated in the story.

Equipment: None

Description:

Skipping and galloping are often difficult locomotor skills for elementary school children to master. This method of teaching these two skills is preceded by a story called "Mr. Selfish meets Ms. Share." The story, which distinguishes between being selfish and sharing, can be told by the physical educator or by the classroom teacher prior to the class.

Galloping

A. Sam Selfish
  1. Designate one foot as Sam Selfish.
  2. Place a frown sticker on Sam Selfish.
  3. Sam Selfish always has to be first, in the front, or in the lead, when moving.
B. Discuss the concept of selfishness.
C. Demonstrate the following selfish movements:
  1. Hop,
  2. Leap,
  3. Slide.

Skipping

A. Sally Share
  1. Designate both feet as Sally Share.
  2. Put a smile sticker on each foot.
  3. Sally Share takes turns when moving.

B. Discuss sharing.

C. Demonstrate and practice sharing movements.
   1. Walk,
   2. Run,
   3. Jump.

ANIMAL CRACKERS

Object: To have children line up according to the sizes of animals depicted on picture cards.

Equipment: Picture cards of animals.

Description:

Divide the class into groups of five to ten, depending on the ages of the students. Have each student pick up a card that has a picture or name of an animal. The students are not to know the names of the other students' animals.

On the teacher's signal, the students line up according to the size of their animal by using only the animal's sound for a clue as to what animal each child represents.

Variations:

1. Cards representing different types of transportation can be used. Have students line up according to the speed of the examples that are used (car, airplane, train, truck, steamboat). This could be used effectively when the students are studying a unit on transportation.

2. Have cards of animals, plants, sports, or some other category that has movement associated with it. On a group or class basis, guess what each child represents by watching his or her movement.

BRIDGE PARTNER

Object: To complete the movement challenges correctly.

Equipment: None

Description:

Each child has a partner during this activity. One partner forms a bridge by using different body parts. The other child finds as many different ways as possible to go under the bridge. The partners then switch positions.

Variations:

1. Vary the challenge. How many ways can you go over the bridge? How many ways can you go around the bridge?
2. Different kinds of bridges will contribute to a variety of techniques that will be used to go over, under, through and around the bridge.
3. A good wind-down at the end of this activity is to have each child demonstrate a special technique they used to go over, around, or under the bridge.

MAGIC BOX

Object: To form, with the body, the shape of an object pulled from the magic box.

Equipment: Any object that has movement. (Examples: balls, nail clippers, rope, teapot, hammer, spray cans, rubber band, drumsticks, etc.) A large box in which to place all the objects.

Description:

The instructor reaches into the box and pulls out an object. The children are asked to form the shape of the object with their bodies. They are then asked to move like the object.

Variations:

1. The children reach into the box and imitate the objects they pull out. They then exchange their objects with each other.
2. Children can be placed in groups and together work out the shape of the objects and their movements in front of the rest of the class.

OVERHEAD PROJECTOR

PROJECTION EXCITEMENT

Note: It is best to use two or more overhead projectors to provide more space for movement.

Object: To have the students move their shadows on the wall while meeting the challenges of varied games and activities.

Descriptions:

Body Awareness

The students watch their shadows on the wall as they run, jump, glide, leap, etc. Students feel free to move since their attention is focused on the shadows instead of themselves The students can respond to all types of problems. How tall can you make yourself? How small? How round? How thin? How high can you jump? How can you become bigger? How can you become smaller?

Feelings

Students can use the overhead projector to depict various feelings through shadows. Anger, hate, fear, love and frustration are examples.

Variations:

1. Let the students select different feelings that they have experienced.
2. Use different colors of clear plastic to express different moods and feelings.

All American

Let the children demonstrate their favorite sport or sport hero or heroine.

Variations:

1. Have the teacher or students select a specific sport or sport skill for the entire class to portray.
2. Have group portrayals.

Red Brick Road

Place a road on the wall with tape or chalk. Have students use the shadows of their heads as cars and follow the road on the wall. Have the road going in different directions and at different heights.

Monster Land

Creepy crawlers are placed on the overhead projector. Children jump, crawl, and change their shadow heights to keep from being touched by the monster.

Variations:

1. Place coins of various sizes at different spots on the overhead projector. Have children jump from one coin to the next as they move their shadows across the wall. They can use a different body part for each trip.
2. Put striking and cutting objects on the overhead. The object of this game is to move about without being stabbed, smashed, or cut.

Murals

Group the students and develop murals on the wall by combining their shadows. This can be open-ended or the teacher can start by making suggestions. Various themes can be used or the mural can be correlated with the topic being studied in another class.

Variations:

1. Let the entire class form both a moving and motionless picture.
2. Add music. Have the students move to the music and then freeze when the music is stopped.

Fish

Place a clear plastic or glass dish of water on the overhead projector. Place creepy crawlers or toy fish in the dish and move it periodically. Students try to swim from one end of the pond to the other while avoiding contact with the creepy crawlers or fish.

Variation:

Have children catch fish. Have children mimic actions of crawlers or fish.

ROPES

ROPE CHALLENGES

Object: To provide a variety of movement challenges through the use of ropes.

Equipment: A rope for each student.

Description:

There are many movement experiences that you can provide for your students through the medium of ropes. Allow them to try the following challenges and then let them experiment with other ways of using their ropes.

A. Lay the rope in the shape of a circle on the ground or floor.
   1. See if you can get inside the circle without touching the rope.
   2. Sit down inside the circle without touching or going over the edge of the rope.
   3. Lie down inside the circle.
   4. Assume another position inside the circle.
   5. Make believe you are in a can and try to push out on the sides (isometrics).
   6. Sit on your bottom with your legs extended out straight; see if you can move yourself in a circular motion without touching the rope with your legs.
   7. Stand, straddle the rope, and see if you can walk around the circle without touching the rope.
   8. Try the same while hopping, skipping, running, jumping, crab walking, etc.
   9. See if you can make a bridge with your stomach facing the rope; with your back to the rope.
   10. See if you can do all in 8. above, backwards.

B. See if you can make your rope into a number 1,2,3, etc.; a snake; a square; a triangle; the first initial of your name, school, etc.; the last initial of your name, school, etc.; another animal; a light bulb; a boat; a football, basketball, tennis ball, a tennis racket, etc.

C. With the rope laid in a straight line on the floor, can you walk it as if it were a tight rope?
   1. Can you do this while moving backward?
   2. Who can walk the tightrope with eyes shut?
   3. Can you jump from side to side across the rope without touching the rope?
   4. Show me if you can hop from side to side without touching the rope.
   5. How else can you move along the rope with your feet without touching the rope? Try a new idea each time.
   6. Can you straddle the rope, jump into the air, turn around, and land on your feet straddling the rope?
   7. How far around can you spin and land on your feet while straddling the rope?
   8. Can you crisscross your hands and feet without touching the rope as you travel along its length?
   9. Can you do this while moving backward?
   10. What other movement pattern can you invent in which you use your hands and feet while moving along the rope without touching it?
D. Make several little circles with your rope. Can you put one body part in each circle and balance? Can you do this while using body parts you didn't use last time?

BLINDFOLD TOUCH

Object: To identify a piece of physical education equipment using only the sense of touch.

Equipment: A blindfold for each child; clothesline rope and various pieces of equipment.

Description:
The rope is tied at various points throughout the gym, approximately three feet off the floor. (Chairs or equipment standards can be used.) The children are blindfolded and start at different places on the rope. Pieces of physical education equip-

ment are placed at various stopping points along the rope. (These stopping points are marked by a piece of tape on the rope.) Each child tries to identify the equipment by using the sense of touch.

Variations:

1. Have partners record the equipment that the blindfolded child guesses.
2. Develop the kinesthetic sense by following the rope through a multidirectional maze while blindfolded.

JUMP AND BOUNCE

Object: To score points by successfully bouncing and catching a basketball a designated number of times while jumping rope.

Equipment: A long jump rope and basketball for each team.

Description:

The class is divided into teams of six to eight members. Teams compete to see who can score the most points. Two players on each team turn the rope while the other members of the team take turns jumping into the middle of the turning rope. The first jumper bounces the ball once, the second jumper twice, etc. When a jumper fails to bounce the ball the required number of times, the next jumper starts with one bounce. A team's inning consists of three jumping opportunities for each player. One point is awarded for each successful bounce of the basketball. (Alternate rope jumpers so every student gets to jump.)

Variation:

Use other hand skills while jumping, such as tossing the ball in the air, passing the ball to a teammate, etc.

ROPE CARDS

Object: To successfully complete the rope task cards.

Equipment: Task cards, jump ropes.

Description:

Design a variety of task cards with rope activities. Place the task cards on the wall and have groups of five to seven students complete the task given on each card. The groups can rotate on a timed basis, or, if there are sufficient task cards, they can move to another card when they complete a task.

Examples of Tasks

1. Jump; hop–left foot, right foot, alternating feet.
2. Move along the floor in a designated pattern. Also backwards.
3. "Pepper"—turn the rope as rapidly as possible.
4. Jump rope moving in the opposite direction.
5. Cross and uncross arms.
6. Have one large rope with each partner turning an end. Jump two at once. (Figure 1-2.)
7. Jump with half turns. (Figure 1-3.)
8. Double Dutch (Backwards) (Figure 1-4.)
9. Triples (very difficult) (Figure 1-5.)

FIGURE 1-2.
Partners jumping with one rope

FIGURE 1-3. Jumping with half turns

FIGURE 1-4. Double Dutch jumping

FIGURE 1-5. Triples jumping

Variations:

1. Have the students create new tasks and make new task cards for their classmates.

2. Have partner and group rope activities as well as individual activities.

PARACHUTES

BEAN BAG WEAVE

Object: To weave in and out of as many people as possible and retrieve the bean bag before the parachute drops.

Equipment: Parachute and bean bag.

Description:

Divide your class into two teams. Allow students to become familiar with raising and lowering the parachute. Place a bean bag under the middle of the parachute. As the parachute is raised by Team 1, a player from Team 2 weaves in and out, through the players on the opposite team in an attempt to get in and out through as many as possible. The player who is running must judge

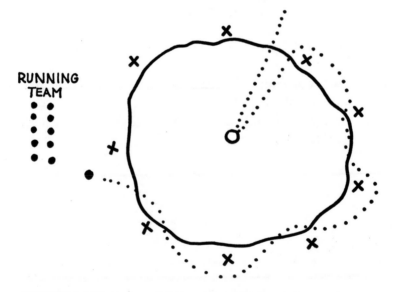

FIGURE 1-6. Pattern to follow when playing Bean Bag Weave

how many players he or she can weave between before picking up the bean bag. The bean bag must be picked up and the player must get his *entire* body out from under the parachute before it drops and touches him. The parachute is held at all times, but it must drop at its own speed, without being pulled down. The students who are running score a point for every person they can pass, provided they get out from under the parachute before it comes down. If the player does not make it out in time, no points are awarded. A running score for each team will be kept, and after the last player on Team 2 finishes, the teams switch. The team with the highest number of points wins.

PARACHUTE GOLF

Object: To score points by being the first team to get its playground ball in the hole in the center of the parachute.

Equipment: Parachute and two playground balls.

Description:
Two teams are designated. Each team holds half of the parachute. Both teams have a ball placed on the parachute and attempt to get their ball in the center hole. The team scoring the most points within the designated time limit is the winner.

Variation:
Have a nine- or eighteen-hole match play contest. The side getting its ball in first wins the hole.

STUNT TIME

Object: To perform the designated stunts before the parachute drops.

Equipment: Parachute.

Description:
Have the students number off by fives. The instructor will designate a stunt to be performed under the parachute. An umbrella will be formed with the parachute. The instructor will call out a number, and all students with that number will run under the parachute to perform the stunt and return before the umbrella falls.

Stunt examples: jump three times; turn around two times and clap your hands three times; sing a nursery rhyme, etc.

Variations:

1. Let the students select a stunt to do.
2. Use mathematics problems to determine which students run under the umbrella.

PARATROOPER

Object: To catch the most beanbags or balls in a designated time limit.

Equipment: Parachute, bean bags, foam rubber balls, or small playground balls.

Description:

The first paratrooper kneels in the center of the parachute. The remainder of the class holds the rim of the parachute. As the balls or beanbags are placed on the parachute, the class shakes the parachute, causing the balls or beanbags to pop up. The player in the center must remain on his knees, but attempts to catch as many balls or beanbags as possible. A thirty-second to one-minute time limit can be used. A bonus can be given if a player catches all the balls or beanbags. The game can also be played in teams, where the people popping up the equipment are on the same team as the paratrooper; then the teams switch.

FIGURE 1-7. Position of students when playing Paratrooper

PARACHUTE VOLLEYBALL

Object: To score the most points by making good shots or causing the opponents to miss shots.

Equipment: One ball.

Description:

A line is painted across the diameter of the parachute. A team stands on each side of the line holding the parachute. The game is played with volleyball rules with the center line representing the net. The serve is made by placing the ball on the outside edge near the center of the serving team. The teams attempt to pop the ball over the net. To increase the difficulty, two or more hits can be required on each side of the "net." (Figure 1-8.)

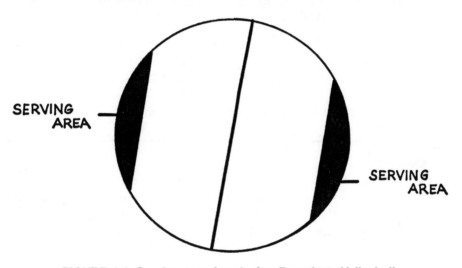

FIGURE 1-8. Serving area for playing Parachute Volleyball

Variations:

1. Divide the circle into quarters and have four teams play. The ball can be returned to any of the other quarter sections. (Figure 1-9.)

2. Tennis can also be played by allowing only one hit before the ball is returned.

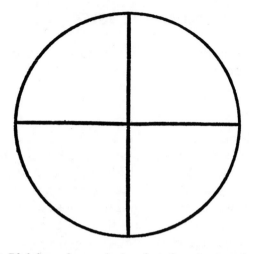

FIGURE 1-9. Division of parachute when four teams play Parachute Volleyball

POISONOUS SNAKES

Object: To avoid being touched by the poisonous snakes.

Equipment: Pieces of rope (without handles), parachute.

Description:
Divide the class into two teams holding onto the parachute. Place the ropes on the parachute and have the students shake it. If a poisonous snake touches a player on the opposing team, that team gets a point against them. The lowest score is the winning one.

SCOOTERS

SCOOTER PUNCHBALL

Object: To score the most goals by punching the foam rubber ball into the goal.

Equipment: Scooters and foam rubber balls.

Description:

Players are distributed throughout the gym on scooters, with one team on each side of the gym. The game starts with a center jump and then the students can move about freely. The object is to move the ball into the goal by punching it with a fist. Only the goalie, who is also on a scooter, is allowed to catch the ball. No player may throw the ball.

SCOOTERBALL

Object: To score points by getting the ball in the trash can while riding on a scooter.

Equipment: Nine scooters per team–eighteen total; two large trash cans; one volleyball or eight-inch playground ball.

Description:

Teams

nine people per team
four defenders
four attackers (shooters)
one rover

Basic Rules

1. The defenders and shooters must stay on their own half of the court. The rover is permitted anywhere on the court.
2. All members must remain on their scooters.
3. Two points are scored from the field. One point is scored for each basket scored from the ten-foot line.
4. Only members in the offensive end can score points, except for foul shots. The players should be switched from offense and defense.
5. Fouls:
   a. Pulling a scooter out from under a player–two shots.
   b. Hitting someone shooting the ball–two shots.
   c. Holding onto a player–one shot.
   d. Leaving the scooter or standing up–one shot.

The Play

1. A bounce tap at center court starts the game.
2. The game follows fundamental basketball play, with each team passing and moving the ball, trying to score a basket while protecting its own goal. (Dribbling can be required for older children.)
3. Any ball played out of bounds will be thrown in by the other team.
4. Fouls are shot from behind the ten-foot line. Only two players from each team are allowed in the semicircle for the rebound.
5. The basket should be placed against a wall to give the shooter a backboard.

Values

1. The children can use some of the basic basketball skills without having to shoot at a high target.
2. It gives the children a chance to work in a different environment. They assume a low-to-the-ground position rather than their normal upright position. It also requires agility to move on wheels rather than use basic locomotor patterns.

3. It is a good lead-up to basketball.

4. It provides a change of pace from basketball.

5. Team play is encouraged.

6. It gives all children a chance to succeed at basketball skills.

Variation:

Scooterball can be adapted to soccer, handball and football.

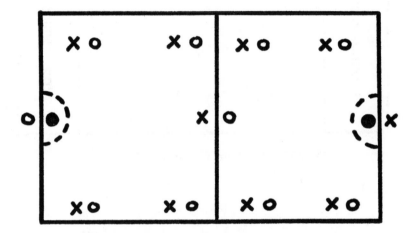

FIGURE 1-10. Player positions for Scooterball

ROLLER BALL

Object: To score the most points by rolling the scooters into the scoring zones.

Equipment: A long mat, approximately five feet by thirty feet; six scooters.

Description:

This game is patterned after shuffleboard. Each player tries to roll scooters into the scoring zone on the mat and knock out the opponent's scooters that are in the scoring zone.

Participants push the scooters with one or two hands while kneeling. Hands may not extend over the foul line. Participants take turns rolling. Three points are awarded for each scooter in the scoring zone that has all four wheels on the mat. (A scooter that leaves the mat with one or more wheels is removed.) Each participant will roll three scooters each turn. Two or four can play.

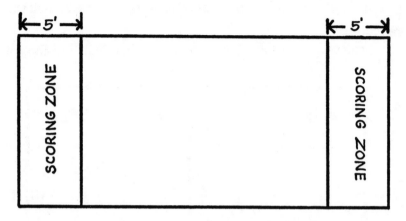

FIGURE 1-11. Court for playing Roller Ball

HOOPS

HULA CONTORTION

Object: To go through the maze of hoops using designated movements.

Equipment: Different-colored hula hoops; a whistle.

Description:

Divide the class into small groups of five to ten children. In each group give all the children a hula hoop, with the exception of one child. Allow the children a few minutes to arrange themselves and their hoops in an unusual position. When the whistle blows, the children hold their position. The child who does not have a hoop must go through all the hoops using different movements such as crawling, rolling and going backwards. Give each child an opportunity to go through the hoops.

HOOP NUMBERS

Object: To walk the shape of the designated number while remaining in the hoops.

Equipment: Hula hoops.

Description:

Each student is given two hoops to lay side by side on the floor. The teacher then calls out a number and the child walks the outline of the number while staying within the two hoops. (Figure 1-12.)

Variations:

1. Outline the letters of the alphabet in the same manner
2. Use different forms of locomotion while outlining numbers or letters.

FIGURE 1-12.
Sample patterns of numbers

HOOP TROOP

Object: To successfully complete the obstacle course as many times as possible in a designated time period.

Equipment: Two fold-up mats; six hoops; one rope; one table or tunnel of some type.

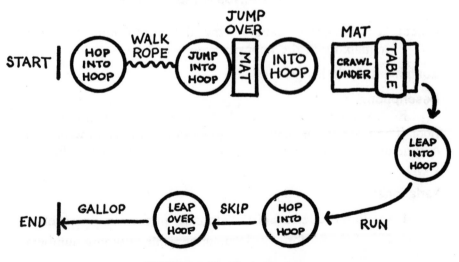

FIGURE 1-13. Obstacle course

Description:
Set up the course as shown and have students go through it as often as possible in the given time. They may score a point for themselves each time they go through the course with no mistakes. The next child may start as soon as the first has jumped over the mat into the hoop. Having no more than five or six students per course gives maximum activity without waiting in line too long.

SCOOTER SCATTER

Object: To be the last set of partners to be tagged.

Equipment: One scooter per player.

Description:
The game is played with partners in a confined area. Partners sit on their own scooters and hook inside arms. One set of partners is "IT" and on the signal they tag other sets of partners using their outside arms only. The tagged partners then join the line at either end. Again they attempt to tag others using only the two outside players' unhooked arms to tag. If the line breaks, they must rejoin before tagging anyone else. The last set of partners tagged is the winner.

FIGURE 1-14. Partner position for playing scooter scatter

ROUND-UP

Object: To lasso the boxes and pull them over the foul line scoring as many points as possible in the designated time limit.

Equipment: Various sizes of empty cardboard boxes or milk crates, each assigned a point value (drawn on the box or crate with magic marker, etc.); clothesline or jumping ropes; hula hoops.

Description:

Set the boxes up so that they are a good distance apart. The player receives a lasso (a hoop with a rope tied to it long enough to reach the farthest box) and stands behind the designated foul line. On a signal, the player attempts to lasso the boxes and pull them across the line. Points are indicated on the boxes. Players may continue to pull boxes across the line until the time limit is up. The player with the most points is the winner. A bonus may be awarded to a player who pulls all the boxes over the line within the time limit.

Variations.

1. Have several students play at the same time.
2. Teams can be designated to compete against one another.

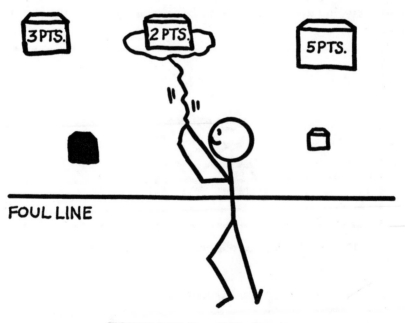

FIGURE 1-15. Round-Up diagram

BOMBS AWAY

Object: To score points by landing a hit (tossing a beanbag into the other team's combat zone.) The first team to land fifteen hits, or the team with the least number of points against them after a time limit, is the winner.

Equipment: One bomb (bean bag) per person; one combat zone (hoop) per person.

Description:

The game is best played in groups of six (three players per team). Players line up across from each other about five yards apart. Each player stands in a hoop and holds one beanbag. On the signal, the players toss the beanbags (underhand only) into the other team's hoops. Players may bat the beanbags before they land in their zones or they may catch them and toss them back. Points are scored each time a beanbag hits the floor inside the combat zone. A scorekeeper can be assigned for each team; he counts the number of hits against that team. When fifteen hits are made, the scorekeeper should signal the end of the game.

Players may leave their zone to pick up beanbags that have landed outside the combat zone and for that time period their zone is unguarded.

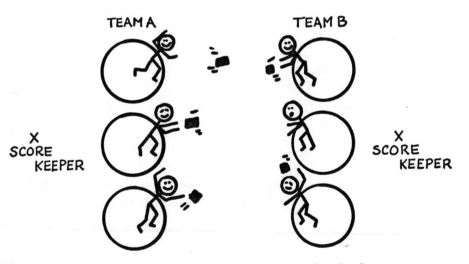

FIGURE 1-16. Team positions for playing Bombs Away

HOOP TOSS

Object: To score points by tossing the hoop over the cone or tossing the hoop closest to the cone. The first to score twenty-one or more points wins the round.

Equipment: Two traffic cones or two milk crates for each set of partners; two hoops per person.

Description:

Each person receives similar hoops. (If you do not have different-colored hoops, then wrap a piece of tape around each person's hoop to distinguish them). Both players start at the same cone and alternate tossing the hoops in an attempt to score points. After all four hoops are tossed, the score is determined, and the partner who tossed second now tosses first. Play continues until one partner reaches twenty-one. If a time limit is used, the winner is the person with the highest score at the end of the time period.

Points are scored as follows:

1. Ringer–The hoop is completely surrounding the cone (three points).

2. Leaner–The hoop is touching or leaning against the cone (two points).

3. Closest hoop–If after both partners have tossed the hoops and both of Partner A's hoops are closer to the cone than both of Partner B's, Partner A receives two points. If only one hoop is closer, one point is awarded.

4. If two ringers are scored by the same person, then six points are awarded.

5. If each partner scores a ringer, only the last ringer counts and negates the other points.

6. If three ringers are scored, the player with two ringers receives three points.

7. It is possible to knock down leaners with the hoops and the score should be determined only after all four hoops have been tossed.

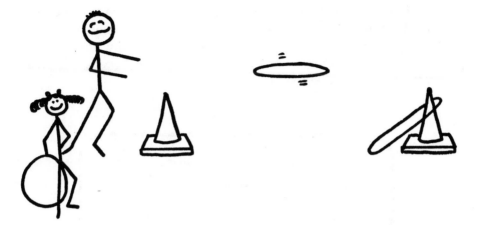

FIGURE 1-17. Positions of players and cones when playing Hoop Toss

SHUFFLE BALL

Object: To score the most goals by knocking down the opposing team's pins.

Equipment: One hoop per person; four pins; one playground ball.

Description:
Each player stands in a hoop that is lying flat on the ground, and must move around the floor without stepping out of the hoop (a shuffling movement works best). Each team has a goalie who guards two pins about ten feet apart. The goalie is protected by a zone that no other player may enter (use cones to designate). The players passing the balls to their teammates get into position to toss the ball and knock down the pins. The players can shuffle while holding the ball in their hands, but they cannot dribble. Players may hold the ball no longer than three seconds before passing or shooting. Knocking down a pin is a goal and scores one point. The pin remains down and is not turned upright unless both pins are hit.

Penalties. If the goalie steps out of the hoop, the opposing team gets one free shot from ten yards in front of the crease

If a player steps out of the hoop, the ball is given to the other team for a free pass. No goal can be scored from this. The winner is the team with the most points at the end of the time limit.

Note: This game can be easily played by four to six people on a team, on half a basketball court.

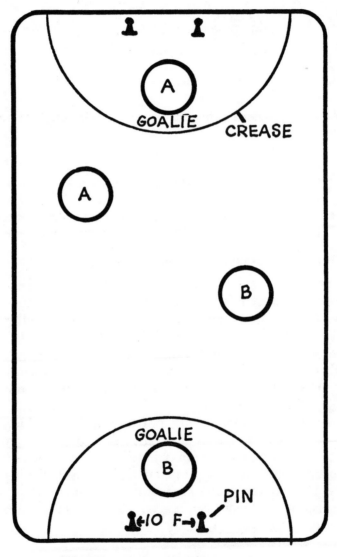

FIGURE 1-18. Shuffle Ball Court Area

NOVELTY APPROACHES

SHOE TIE TIME

Object: To learn to tie shoelaces correctly.

Equipment: Coffee cans with plastic tops; shoelaces.

Description:

Shoe-tying skill is often lacking in kindergarteners and first graders. This game is designed to develop finger dexterity and to decrease the amount of class time that is spent in tying shoes.

The coffee cans are made into shoe-tying cans by punching two holes in the plastic lid with a paper punch, and then stringing a shoelace through the top. The plastic top is then snapped back on the can and the children are shown the relationship between tying the lace on the can and tying their own shoes. After everyone has mastered tying, the children can play relay games for a class activity.

Variation:

Similar games can be developed for zippers and buttons.

STRAIGHT JACKET

Object: This game has a variety of purposes and can be used with different grade levels. It provides an opportunity for students to learn to give explicit directions, and it develops listening skills. It helps younger children learn the parts of the body and learn direction; right from left, up, down, front, and back.

Equipment: One jacket.

Description:

Begin the game by putting the jacket on the floor. The students then tell the teacher how to put on the jacket. Each student takes a turn and may give one and only one direction at a time. The game continues until the jacket is put on correctly.

Variations.

1. Group the students and have one student in each group put on the jacket.
2. Use other items of apparel such as gloves, sweat pants, or a ski cap.

RIGHT, LEFT, LEFT, RIGHT

Object: To develop use of the nondominant side of the body.

Equipment: None.

Description:

This technique is particularly effective with students who seem to have reached a plateau of skill development in a sports activity. Frequently, the execution of a skill has become an automatic response and the student is unable to intellectualize the components of the skill in order to continue to improve. With this technique, the student is asked to use his or her nondominant side to execute the same skill. This forces the student to analyze the skill and the increased insight will usually be applied to skill execution when the student again uses the dominant side.

This approach to teaching is valuable for all age levels so children will learn to effectively use their nondominant side. This is important for well-rounded motor development.

Variations:

1. Play games requiring the use of the nondominant side.
2. Provide scoring differentials in a game. For example, double the score value when a basket or goal is made with the nondominant hand or foot.

CREATIVE MIMICRY IN SCHOOL AND PLAYGROUND SAFETY

Object: To emphasize good safety skills in the playground.

Equipment: None.

Description:

This class should be one of the first classes each year. Begin the class by emphasizing that school and playground safety is *very important*. Give each child a slip of paper and ask the class to think of a safety tip for school or playground safety. After giving the children a few minutes to think, have them print the proper or positive safety procedure to follow. Give each child the opportunity to pantomime his or her safety tip in front of the class, and have the members of the class attempt to guess what it is. The teacher may need to go around the class as the students are writing, and provide suggestions for safety tips to avoid duplication. Careful guidance will be necessary to help students think of appropriate safety procedures.

The purpose of printing the safety tips is to incorporate practice in spelling.

2

Tag, You're It!

Low-Organization Games
and Variations
to Maintain Enthusiasm
in Your Classes

Games provide enjoyment for all ages. It is good to take a hint from the backyard activities of children and include games that have a minimum of structure in the lower elementary grades. This type of game is fun, provides plenty of challenges, and stimulates the children to improvise. The opportunity for student creativity is a very important characteristic of low-organization games. In addition, children have the opportunity to develop basic fundamental skills and begin to understand the application of rules and regulations to the play of group games.

Traditional games should be one part of the school's curriculum. It is also important to have original games that will incorporate both cooperative and competitive elements of play. Selecting new games and developing original and creative twists to traditional games provides a needed balance to keep children motivated and challenged.

Original games can be developed by the teacher, by students or by the teacher and students working together. The teacher can provide a game framework and let the students make changes and modifications; or the students can be given items of equipment to use in making up a game. Either approach will result in numerous, excellent games of low organization which the students will thoroughly enjoy because they are *their games*.

To increase your program, we have included new games for you to use. Take the traditional games and the new games found in this chapter and modify them to further increase the scope of your program. Games can be changed by varying the formations used, incorporating different equipment, using different scoring procedures changing from a competitive to a cooperative game, increasing or decreasing the number of players, using partners, varying boundaries and distances, adding obstacles and/or using a different form of locomotion. After your students have had experience modifying games, let them design their own games. You will now have all the ingredients that are needed for a successful unit devoted to games of low organization. Changing games and creating new ones is an excellent way to increase interest and enthusiasm, and brings versatility and adaptability to the process of game play.

NEW GAMES

SUPERSHOES

Object: To be the first team to spell out "supershoes" by getting one of the four sneakers and returning to the line before the other teams.

Equipment: Four sneakers.

Description:

Four teams line up around the periphery of the gymnasium, using the endlines and sidelines. Four sneakers are placed in the center. The students on each team are given a number which corresponds to a number on the other teams. When a number is called out, the players must run around the outside of the formation in a clockwise direction, enter through their empty spot, grab a sneaker, and return it to their spot. When the person returns with the sneaker, all team members must sit down and yell "supershoes." The first team back gets two letters in spelling "supershoes" and the second team gets one letter. The first team to spell out "supershoes" is the winner.

Variation:

Use other equipment such as a basketball and have the person getting the basketball dribble it through a designated route.

FOLLOW ME

Object: To increase the concentration of the class during group instruction.

Equipment: None.

Description:

The instructor or leader will face the group and be visible to everyone. The action will consist of body movements. The class is to follow closely the leader's movements. This techinque can be used at any time during warm-ups or for formal instruction in an activity. The technique is greatly improved if the instructor can "ham it up" while performing the movements. Through this exercise, the instructor demonstrates the importance of following directions to learn a physical skill.

HIDDEN TREASURE

Object: To accumulate the most points by finding golf balls that have been given different values.

Equipment: Golf balls of different colors.

Description:

Hide approximately 100 multicolored golf balls at some location within walking distance. Hike with the children to the spot where the golf balls have been hidden. Allow fifteen to twenty minutes for the children to find the golf balls. Each color has a different point value so that the next task is for each child to tabulate the number of points the golf balls represent.

Variations:

1. Use teams of two, three, four, or five, and see which team can accumulate the most points.
2. Place a team container some distance from the hiding spot. Any time a golf ball is found, the finder must run and deposit it in the container.
3. Different forms of locomotion can be used when searching for a golf ball or after finding one.

CRAZY BALL

Object: To develop eye-hand coordination by using throwing, catching, and bouncing skills.

Equipment: A racquetball or tennis ball for each child in the class.

Description:

Each student takes a ball and moves to any area of the gym. The activity consists of having the children throw, bounce, and catch their balls any way they like. They are encouraged to use walls, baskets and other equipment in the gym. Emphasis is placed on using available space without running into anyone else.

Variations:

1. Alternate between using dominant and nondominant hands.

2. Use a variety of different-sized balls. Every two minutes, have the students obtain a different ball to throw, bounce, or catch.

TAG

STEAL THE TIRE

Object: To get the tire across your team's line before being tagged.

Equipment: One used tire.

Description:
Line up two equal teams on the sidelines of the gymnasium. Have the players on each team numbered. Place a tire in the center of the gym. Follow the same rules as for Steal the Bacon by having the students whose numbers are called run out to get the tire and bring it back across their sideline before they can be tagged. The tire must be carried or rolled under control to the sideline.

Variation:
Call two or more numbers so strategy can be used by rolling the tire to a teammate in order to get the tire back before being tagged.

COOKIE MONSTER

Object: To avoid being tagged by the "cookie monster."

Equipment: None.

Description:
One player is the cookie monster and the other players are the cookies. The cookie monster is in a hut (designated area in one end of the gym) and the cookies are in the cookie box, which is located in another part of the gym. The cookies approach the monster and keep asking if he is hungry. When the monster yells, "I'm Hungry," he chases the cookies. All cookies tagged before they reach the cookie box become cookie monsters. The game continues until there are no cookies left.

DRIBBLE TAG

Object: To dribble a basketball while tagging other players, and avoid being tagged yourself.

Equipment: One basketball or any type of ball for each student.

Description:

Each student is dribbling a basketball. Have six to eight students in each group. All members of the group must stay within a designated area. Each player tries to tag other players while dribbling his or her basketball. Players may not tag the person who tagged them. A player gets one point for every player tagged.

Variation:

Have two-minute periods, and at the end of each period the six players with the most tags form a group to play dribble tag during the next two-minute period.

TAG 'EM

Object: To avoid being tagged by the player who is it, and is throwing the ball at the other players.

Equipment: Foam rubber balls.

Description:

One player is "It" and tries to tag people by hitting them with the ball. When a player is hit, he then becomes "It" and changes places with the former tagger.

Variations:

Each person tagged gets a ball and becomes another "It." Continue until the last player is finally tagged.

BALLS

BALLOON BALL

Object: To successfully complete movement activities using balloons.

Equipment: Blown-up balloons.

Description:

This is a good game to use to develop ball skills for younger children or to provide a change of pace for older students.

Each child is given a balloon and is directed by the teacher's questions and suggestions.

1. How many times can you tap the balloon?
2. Can you keep the balloon up in the air without using your hands?
3. Keep the balloon in the air using only a lower part of your body.
4. Choose a partner and put one balloon down. How long can the two of you keep the balloon in the air?
5. Now tap the balloon back and forth with each partner taking a turn. Count your taps. Now use parts of your body other than your hands to keep the balloon up in the air. See how many different parts of the body you can use to keep the balloon in the air.

CONTAINER BALL

Object: To successfully complete throwing tasks as designated.

Equipment: Different-size balls and containers.

Description:

Each child pairs up with a partner. One partner starts by throwing a big ball into a big container. This is held by the partner. For example, a playground ball and a large basket might be used at first. When they have mastered this level of throwing, they may proceed to the next level which would be a smaller ball thrown into a smaller container, such as a gallon can.

Partners take turns throwing and catching. The partner with the container moves the container to try to catch the ball. This procedure provides success for both the thrower and the catcher.

Variations:

1. Specify the type of throw that will be used.

2. Increase the distance of the throw.

DODGE 'EM

Object: To throw the ball to a partner without hitting the other thrown balls. To exchange places with a partner without contacting another game member.

Equipment: Balls.

Description:

The objective of this game is to develop ball skills and to move through floor space without colliding with other participants. The game utilizes a problem-solving approach. One ball is needed for every two students. The size of the ball depends on the age, skill level, and the progression that is being used. Each student selects a partner. Partners then face each other forming a rectangle.

The game starts with all of the A students throwing the balls to their partners. They can roll, bounce, or toss the ball. Once all the B players get the balls, they set them on the floor and change places with their partners without bumping into each other, or into other students. They will toss the balls back and forth three times and then B will start throwing the ball.

At the end of the game, ask how many times the students bumped into each other, and how many had collisions with their balls. It is also a good learning experience to have the players demonstrate how they got the balls to their partners. The game becomes very sloppy when it is made into a race.

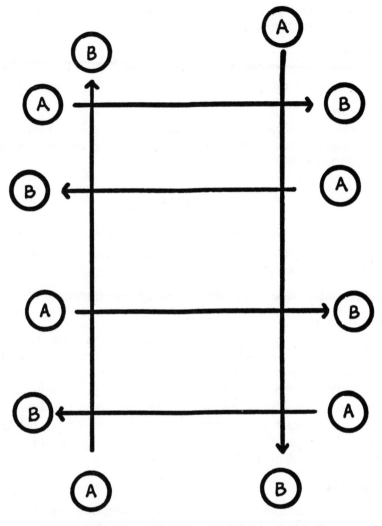

FIGURE 2-1. Player Position for playing Dodge 'Em

PING PONG TENNIS

Object: To score more points than the opponent by causing him to miss the ball or by placing good shots on the court.

Equipment: A paddle for each player and tennis balls for each court; a blacktop surface divided into courts with a net through the middle of the court. (The net height and court size can vary with available equipment and blacktop space.)

Description:

The game is played with table tennis rules. Each team gets five serves and the players must take turns hitting the ball.

Variation:

Play with three or four players on a team. Make a cooperative game and see how many times the ball can be hit back and forth without bouncing twice.

SCATTER

Object: To kick the ball, run around the traffic cone and return home before the fielding team can catch the ball, line up, and pass the ball between their legs.

Equipment: Home plate; playground ball; traffic cone.

Description:

Two equal teams play this game. Only the team in the field can score. The kicker must kick the ball, run around the traffic cone, and return to the home plate before the other team lines up behind the person who caught the ball and passes it between their legs to the person at the end of the line. The fielding team receives one point for each person who touches the ball before the kicker crosses home plate. Each member of the kicking team kicks once, and then the teams exchange positions.

Variations:

1. Have all members of the fielding team freeze when the ball is fielded. The ball must then be thrown to the other members of the team.

2. Instead of throwing the ball, have the receiving team members kick the ball to each other.

3. When a member of the team catches the ball, the other players line up behind the player and pass the ball between their legs. The last person runs to the front of the line and holds the ball overhead. If this is accomplished before the runner scores, they get a point; if not, the runner gets a point.

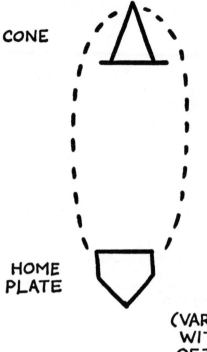

CONE

HOME
PLATE

(VARY THE CONE LOCATION
WITH THE AGE AND SKILL
OF THE PLAYERS.)

FIGURE 2-2. Cone position for Scatter

BOUNDARY BOMBER

Object: To bounce or roll the ball over the other team's goal line.

Equipment: One or more ball(s) per team.

Description:

    Divide the players into two teams. Each team stays on its own half of a court with a center dividing line that may not be crossed by any player. Each team has a goal line behind it which it has to defend by preventing the ball(s) from crossing it. Balls *must* bounce or roll over the goal line.

Variation:

    Use feet only to kick the ball across the goal line.

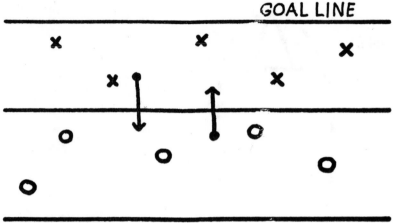

FIGURE 2-3. Field positions for Boundary Bomber

MUSICAL HOT POTATO

Object: To toss the ball around a circle and to avoid being left holding the "potato" when the music stops.

Equipment: A music source—records, record player; playground balls.

Description:

Students form a circle and one player starts the ball. When the music starts, the ball is tossed around the circle. When the music stops, the ball is held. The student left holding the potato receives a "p" for the first letter in potato. Each time someone is left holding the ball, she receives a letter. When "potato" is spelled out, the game starts over.

Variations:

1. Rather than receiving letters, students must perform skills to get themselves back into the game.

2. Use more than one ball.

ROLLERBALL

Object: To stay in the circle as long as possible and avoid having the ball hit you.

Equipment: One or more foam rubber or playground balls.

Description:

Divide the class into two equal groups and have one group form a circle with the other group inside. The players forming the circle try to roll the ball(s) to hit the feet of their opponents. When players are hit, they are out and wait outside the circle until the time is up or until all the players are out. The teams then change positions.

Variation:

When players are hit, they join the circle and the last player out is the winner.

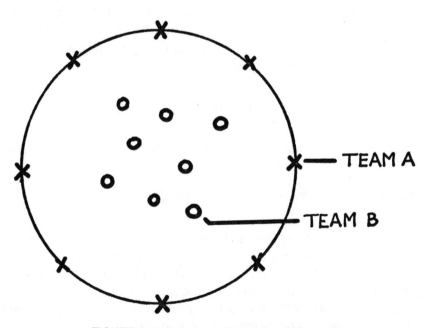

FIGURE 2-4. Player positions for Rollerball

GETTING TO KNOW YOU

Object: To get to know the names of the members in your group while tossing a ball to those members.

Equipment: Playground ball.

Description:

Form a circle. One person starts the ball and tosses or rolls it to another player. The person who has the ball first says his own name then the name of the player who is to receive the ball. Play continues in this manner.

Variations:

1. Have the students say their own names, then the names of every player while tossing the ball to each player. Allow each child to take a turn saying all the names.

2. Say your name, then toss the ball to another player who must say the name of the player who tossed the ball, then add her name to the sequence. Continue until a mistake is made, and start again.

BATTLEBALL

Object: To retrieve a foam rubber ball when your number is called and hit your opponent with it before you are hit.

Equipment: Two foam rubber balls per game.

Description:

Two teams form one circle, each on its own half of a dividing line. Each student on each team is given a number. Place the balls in the center of the circle. The teacher calls a number and one student from each team runs to pick up a ball and tries to hit his opponent before being hit. Other players can get a loose ball and toss it to their center player, but cannot hit the opposing center player themselves. The first center player to hit his opponent gets a point for his team. Players must stay in their own half of the circle.

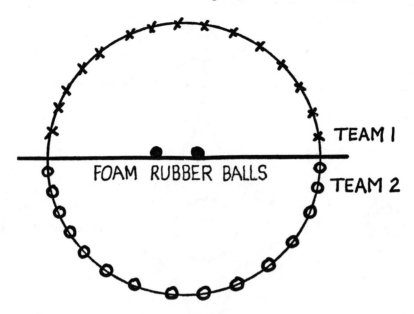

FIGURE 2-5.
Player position for Battleball

EIGHT LEGS

Object: The object of the game is to pass the ball between another player's legs, thereby scoring points.

Equipment: A playground ball for each group of four students.

Description:
The game begins with four players standing in stride position in a square, with a playground ball placed in the middle. On a signal, the players, using their hands only, try to pass the ball between the legs of a teammate. A point is scored each time a player successfully passes the ball through another player's legs.

Variation:
Use different-size balls.

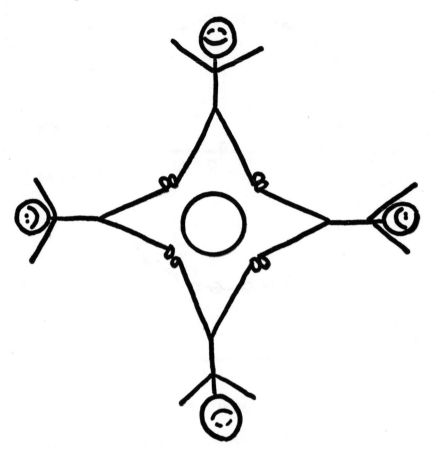

FIGURE 2-6. Stride position of players

BALL FOUR

(Volleyball, Basketball, Baseball, Football)

Object: To score points by crossing home plate before the opposing
team makes a basket.

Equipment: Football; volleyball net; basketball hoop; bases.

Description:

A team is on each side of a volleyball net. One team lines up at
a home plate with a football. The team with the football has one

player at a time kick the football over the net. This player must run around the court and return home before the other team makes a basket with the football. A point is scored each time a runner crosses home plate before a basket is scored. Each player has the opportunity to kick in each inning.

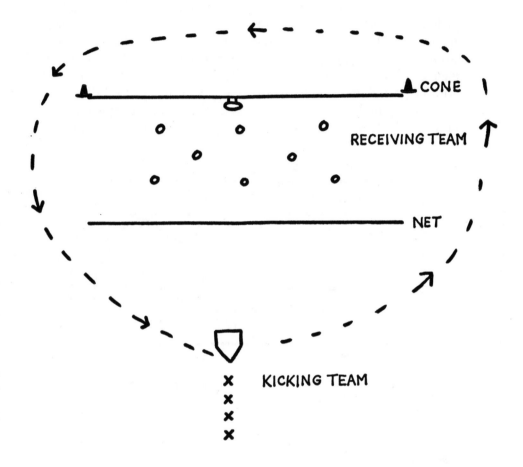

FIGURE 2-7. Court set-up for playing Ball Four

Variation:

Have the receiving team pass the ball to each member of the team rather than shoot a basket.

PASS-IT BASKETBALL

Object: To practice passing, dribbling and shooting skills.

Equipment: Cones; basketballs.

Description:

Each member of a team has a number; when the number is called, that individual must throw a two-handed chest pass to each member of his or her team. After passing, the individual must dribble through the cones in a zigzag manner and shoot a lay-up shot at his or her team's basket. Points are awarded for passing without mistakes, or without missing a cone when dribbling, and for making the lay-up shot. This game emphasizes team work, and all individuals on both teams are actively involved in the game.

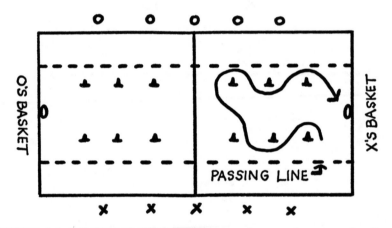

FIGURE 2-8. Diagram of player positions and cone placement for Pass-It Basketball

Variations:

1. Increase the number of balls until only one person is on the sidelines receiving the passes and the rest are dribbling or shooting.
2. Require alternating hands when dribbling.
3. Use the nondominant hand.
4. Use different types of shots.

KNEE KICKBALL

Object: To score points by making a basket or preventing a partner from making a basket.

Equipment: Playground ball or foam rubber ball.

Description:
Each student has a partner. Partners face each other five to eight feet apart. (The distance can be varied to increase the difficulty of the game.) One partner stands with arms extended in a circular pattern in front of the body, with the hands clasped. This forms a human basketball backstop and hoop. The other partner throws the ball into the arms of the other person. As the ball passes through his arms, Partner 1 scores a point if he is successful in kneeing the ball back out of the hoop. Partner 2 scores a point if the ball passes through the hoop and lands on the floor.

BLANKET BALL

Object: To score points by either catching propelled balls or by propelling balls so they land on the floor in bounds.

Equipment: Blanket; balls of different sizes; volleyball net.

Description:
Two or three teams can be used. One team stands on one side of the volleyball net with a blanket covered with balls of many different sizes and shapes. The other team or teams distribute their players on the court on the other side of the net. (A larger playing area can be used if the teams are large.) On the teacher's signal, the balls are propelled over the net with the blanket. Teams get one point for every ball that is caught. The serving team gets one point for every ball that hits the floor in bounds. Any ball landing out of bounds is subtracted from the serving team's score.

Variations:

1. Have the receiving team catch balls with a blanket. Small blankets with four players would be good. Towels can also be used.

2. Make it a cooperative game by using only two or three balls and see how many balls can be caught before a ball touches

the floor. Use the same number of blankets on each side of the net.

HOOP BALL

Object: To successfully throw various types of balls through a suspended hoop.

Equipment: A hoop for each team; all sizes and shapes of balls.

Description:

Hang a hoop from two baskets and place all the balls in the center of the floor. Have one team lined up on each sideline. The players on each team are numbered. When a number is called, the player with that number on each team runs to the balls and throws as many as possible through their team's hoop. Only one ball can be thrown at a time and the ball must be thrown from at least ten feet away. (The minimum distance can be varied with the ages and skills of the children.) One point is received for each ball passing through the hoop in thirty seconds. All team members run to retrieve the balls and place them in the center of the floor.

Variations:

1. Call several numbers at a time.
2. Use different forms of locomotion to go to the balls.
3. Call two numbers and require one pass before the ball is thrown through the hoop.
4. Hang a hoop from more baskets and have more teams.

TEN IN A ROW

Object: Teams try to complete ten passes in a row without having the ball dropped or intercepted.

Equipment: Playground ball for each game.

Description:

An even number of teams are formed, with six to eight players on a team, and teams are paired for competition. The player with the ball is allowed to take two steps before passing, and no body contact is permitted. A dropped or intercepted ball goes to the other team which then begins counting completed passes.

Variations:

1. Use yarn balls, rings, bean bags, or some other type of ball.
2. Change the playing area or locomotor movement that is permitted.
3. Run a round robin or elimination tournament on a timed basis. The teams with the most consecutive successful passes are the winners at the end of the time period.

CORNER HANDBALL

Object: To hit the ball with your hand, causing it to hit the wall and land in bounds so that your partner cannot return it.

Equipment: Handball, racquetball, or tennis ball.

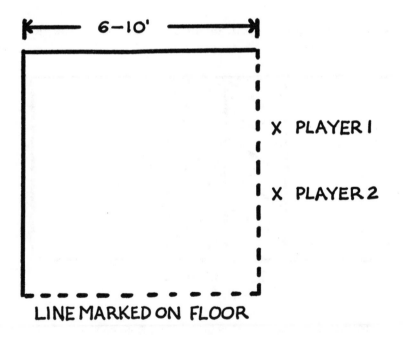

FIGURE 2-9. Court diagram for playing Corner Handball

Description:

This game is played in the corner of the gymnasium or other room. It can be played even if there are some obstructions on the walls. A square playing surface of approximately six to ten feet is adequate. The game begins with a lob serve against the wall that the server is facing. Regular handball rules are used. Both walls may be used as long as the ball lands within the square.

Variations:

1. Doubles can be played.
2. Increase the size of the court and play racquetball.

ONE BOUNCE FREE

Object: To bounce the ball in the opponent's free square area causing it to land in bounds so that it cannot be caught.

Equipment: Playground ball for each game.

Description:

Existing lines can be used, or lines can be put on the floor with tape or floor paint.

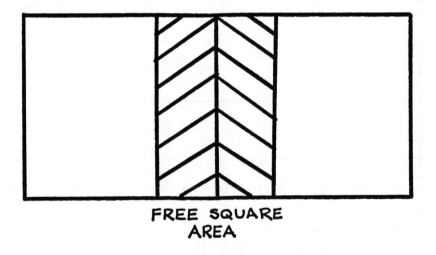

FREE SQUARE AREA

FIGURE 2-10. Diagram of court for One Bounce Free

The player with the ball bounces it into the opponent's free square area. The opponent must catch the ball before it bounces in his or her square. The ball is returned in the same manner. A point is scored if the ball bounces in the opponent's square.

Variations:

1. Vary the size of the playing area.
2. Bat the ball instead of catching and throwing the ball.

GOAL HANDBALL

Object: To hit the ball as in handball—to rebound it off the wall and into the goal which is a box.

Equipment: Handball or tennis ball and a basket or box for each player.

Description:

The players start by dropping their balls and hitting them against the wall. The challenge is to have the ball land in their basket when it rebounds.

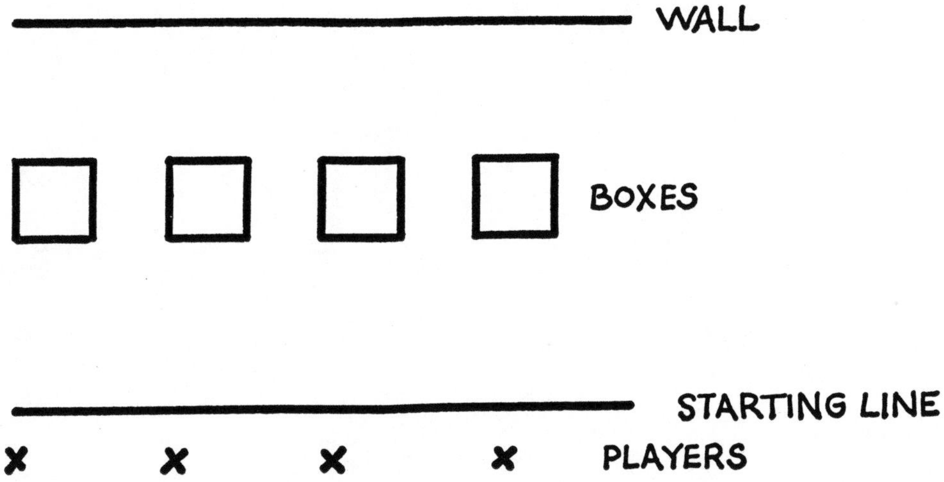

FIGURE 2-11. Player position when playing Goal Handball

Variations:

1. Start with large boxes and gradually decrease the size of the boxes.
2. Let one student try to catch the ball in a box when it comes off the wall.
3. Vary the distance the box is placed from the wall.

OTHER

PAIL TOSS

Object: To score points by tossing beanbags into the opposing team's pail.

Equipment: A belt, beanbag, and pail for each student.

Description:
There are two teams. Each student has a pail attached to her back by a belt. Each team has a different-colored pail and each student has a beanbag of the same color as the pail he or she is wearing. The object of the game is to throw your bean bag into an opponent's pail while keeping your pail empty. The team with the fewest beanbags in their pails at the end of the game gets one point. The first team to get a predetermined number of points is the winner.

Variation:
Have each team throw beanbags into the pail of a teammate. (The distance they would be apart would be determined by the ages and the skills of the students.)

MUSIC MAZE

Object: To perform designated skills correctly when the music stops.

Equipment: A piece of physical education equipment for each student.

Description:
Students use a designated locomotor movement to go around the gym in time to music. When the music stops, each student goes to a piece of equipment using the same locomotor movement. A

designated skill is performed with the piece of equipment until the music starts again. For example, those who go to a basketball might shoot a basket; those who have a hoop will do the hula; those with stilts will walk, etc.

Variation:

Have cardboard posters made to indicate the stunt to be performed at each station when the music stops.

FIT AND FUN GAME

Object: To score points by successfully completing tasks as designated.

Equipment: Four of each of the following: footballs, softballs, basketballs, volleyballs, and tennis rackets.

Description:

Players are divided equally into four teams with each player having a number. When the teacher calls out a number, the player with that number on each team comes out for the game. Two players are called each time. The person with the first number performs the physical fitness skill and the person with the second number does the ball skill.

Physical Fitness Skills	Ball Skills
A. Push-Up	A. Football passing from ten yards to a teammate
B. Squat Thrust	B. Softball pitch from ten yards to a wall target
C. Sit-Ups	C. Tennis volley against the wall
D. Jumping Jacks	D. Soccer dribbling around two cones
E. Six Point Push-Ups	E. Basketball lay-up
F. Choice	F. Repetition of volleyball sets

Team score is determined by the number of times each ball skill and physical fitness skill are performed in one minute. Every minute the teacher calls out two numbers and a letter that stands for two new players and the physical fitness and ball skills that are to be performed.

Variations:

1. Design a spinning wheel that lists a variety of physical fitness and ball skills. Have the competitors spin the wheel to see which skill they are to perform.

2. Call out several numbers if there is sufficient space. This game is excellent as an outside activity. Simply designate outdoor ball skills.

3. Have the students design the skills that will be used in the game.

3

Gee, This Is as Much Fun as Real Basketball

116 Challenging Lead-Up Games and Activities

Lead-up games can be used for any age group. These games are basically modified games that incorporate fundamental skills, techniques, or rules of a game such as basketball or volleyball. They can be stepping stones to the complexities of a full scale game. They permit a player to isolate and practice individual game techniques while at the same time maintaining interest and attention. This does not mean that you will not be teaching the basic skills. Lead-up games are an important part of the learning process because they give students the opportunity to perfect their skills. They are a part of the foundation development which is needed for success in competitive games. In many ways, lead-up games can be considered a bridge between the early elementary years and the game activities included in the physical education curriculum of the upper elementary grades. They make the progression from simple to complex play possible in a positive educational framework.

Lead-up games are relatively easy to learn and understand. This alleviates some of the frustrations of complex games and improves a child's emotional set toward organized physical activity. These games are easy to manipulate so the emphasis on winning can be kept in proper perspective.

It should be emphasized that lead-up games have value in and of themselves. They can be structured so a child at any skill level can learn and enjoy learning. They can be purposeful and rewarding for every student. Progression from simple to complex can be incorporated easily into a curriculum through the use of lead-up games.

Another great characteristic of lead-up games is their flexibility. They can be changed easily to fit skill levels, the variety of skills in a class, facilities and equipment that are available, and the time frame within which a teacher must operate.

Lead-up games are conducive to teaching. They can be structured so instruction is maximized. Their informality permits the teacher to concentrate on teaching sport skills. Because many lead-up games use small numbers of participants in each game, it is easier for the teacher to "tune in" to emotional and social needs as well as those of a physical nature.

Basics can be stressed in lead-up games while at the same time maintaining elements of surprise, self competition and variable outcomes. Lead-up games also lend themselves to combining skills of several different sports. This is another important feature as a student who is oriented toward one sport will be motivated to participate because of interest or skill in that sport. At the same time, skills and strategies of another sport or sports will be learned and this experience frequently leads to interest in additional activities.

Lead-up games can be structured to reduce the "threat" of participating in a new activity. There is no need for a student to feel intimidated by more skilled teammates because lead-up games can provide success for every skill level. They can range from being highly competitive to being totally cooperative. Frequently, a prime characteristic of a lead-up game is self challenge. The opportunity to achieve higher personal goals is a key factor in motivation.

The lead-up games in this chapter will provide many enjoyable and worthwhile activities for your classes. Use these as a guide for designing additional lead-up games. Modify the ones found in this chapter if you want to use different equipment or emphasize a different skill. Remember that lead-up games can easily change with the times. Keep them current with student interests and changing physical education programs.

Lead-up games have many values for both the student and the teacher. They make it possible to have a wide variety of challenging games and they can provide maximum participation in many forms of vigorous activity. They have built-in flexibility potential so all skill levels will receive benefit. An especially important characteristic is the skill progression which lead-up games can encompass. They provide an important transition for children moving from a strictly movement-oriented program to simple games to complex games. This permits children to gain positive experience in team play, in working with a group. Competition can be controlled at a healthy level.

In summary, lead-up games form an important base upon which a student's future activity participation is founded. Personal satisfaction through successful achievement typifies a physical education program that makes proper use of lead-up games.

SOCCER

GOAL CHALLENGE

Object: To score by kicking the soccer ball past the goalie and into the goal.

Equipment: Two soccer balls at each goal.

Description:

Two teams are placed at each goal area. One team stands behind the goal with one member becoming the goalie. The other team stands about twenty yards in front of the goal and has one member attempting to score on the goalie from designated locations on the field. Team members rotate until every person has a turn and then the teams switch positions. Successful goals determine the team scores.

Variations:

1. Have two players on defense (goalie and fullback) and two on offense.
2. Change the distance and angle of the shots.

SIAMESE SOCCER

Object: To kick or throw the ball into the opponent's goal.

Equipment: Soccer ball; material to tie legs together.

Description:

Each player ties one leg to the leg of a teammate. The game begins with the ball on the ground. The ball can be caught only after it is kicked in the air. Only one hand can be used to catch and throw the ball. No goalie is permitted and goals must be scored from a distance of at least ten yards from the goal.

Variations:

1. Use two goals at each end of the field. This will increase the action.
2. Play the game without using hands.
3. Use two or more balls.

SOCCER KEEP AWAY

Object: To keep the ball away from the opposing team using soccer skills.

Equipment: Soccer ball for each group of five players.

Description:
    Three players attempt to keep the ball away from two players by dribbling and passing in a defined area. Players change positions when a ball is intercepted or stolen on a dribble.

Variation:
    Vary the number of players on offense and defense.

POSITION SOCCER

Object: To have every player kick the ball before the team can score a goal.

Equipment: Soccer ball for each team.

Description:
    Have players assume positions in their playing zones. There are no defensive players. The goalie throws or kicks the ball to a teammate. Every player must kick the ball before a goal can be scored.

Variations:

1. Make the game competitive by timing how long it takes to score a goal. Rotate a new team on the field as soon as one team scores.

2. Require a certain type of kick or position on the field in order for a goal to count.

3. Decrease the size of the field.

UP, UP AND AWAY

Object: To practice soccer skills using balloons.

Equipment: Heavy duty round balloons.

Description:

Balloons can be effective teaching aids when teaching lead-up skills. They add sparkle to classes practicing ball skill fundamentals. As an example, soccer kicks such as the instep, side of the foot, and volley can all be practiced with a balloon. The thigh, instep, and chest traps also lend themselves to balloon usage. Throw-ins can also be practiced by painting lines on the balloons to check for spin.

Variation:

Practice ball skills for other sports also; volleyball, basketball, football, etc.

HEADS-UP SOCCER

Object: To head the ball into various zones, thereby scoring points.

Equipment: Soccer ball.

Description:

Two teams of six players take alternate positions on the playing field or court as shown on the following chart. Numbers in the squares indicate the point value for scoring from that square. The goal dimensions can be varied according to available equipment. Two cones can be used for goals for younger players.

The game begins by a jump-off at the center squares. Players must move the ball across the playing area by heading. Goals can be scored only by heading. Each player must remain in his or her square. Any part of the body allowed in soccer may be used to keep the ball in the air, but only the head may be used to move the ball

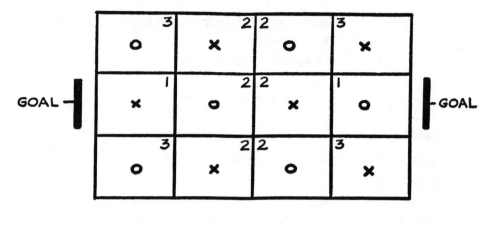

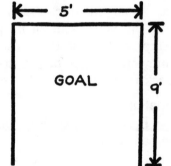

FIGURE 3-1.

Player positions for Heads-Up Soccer

from square to square. A free head is given at the point of out of bounds and at a square where a violation has occurred. Scoring is not allowed on a free head ball.

Variation:

Have a cooperative game with players positioned five or six feet apart. The players work together to head the ball into a goal.

SOCCER BOWLING

Object: To knock as many Indian clubs down as possible, by kicking a ball at them.

Equipment: Soccer balls; Indian clubs or bowling pins; traffic cones.

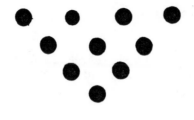

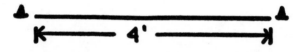

FIGURE 3-2. Soccer Bowling pin placement

Description:

Ten bowling pins or Indian clubs are placed at one end of the gymnasium. Two cones are set four feet apart and twenty feet in front of the clubs.

Set up several stations so that all children will be active. Students try to knock the Indian clubs down by kicking the ball between the cones. Scoring can be the total number of pins knocked down by younger children with regular bowling scoring used by older students.

Variations:

1. Have students dribble to the cones before kicking.
2. Have a partner roll the ball, which must be trapped before kicking.

JUGGLING THREESOMES

Object: To keep the ball in the air by using any body part except the hands and arms.

Equipment: Soccer balls.

Description:

Divide the class in groups of three and give each group a soccer ball. Each team counts the number of successful hits before the ball hits the ground.

Variations:

1. Have different numbers of players in a group.
2. As skills increase, give a ball to each student to see how long each one can keep the ball in the air.
3. Allow only head balls or foot control.

FLAG FOOTBALL

THREE-BALL RECEIVING GAME

Object: To catch footballs being thrown and lobbed from different angles while at the same time learning to run different pass patterns.

Equipment: Footballs and traffic cones.

Description:

The runner receives a pass after cutting through a set of cones. The first two footballs are dropped when approaching the next set of cones and the last football is run back to Passer 1. Each receiver runs the pass patterns four times and then three new passers are designated so everyone has the opportunity to be a passer.

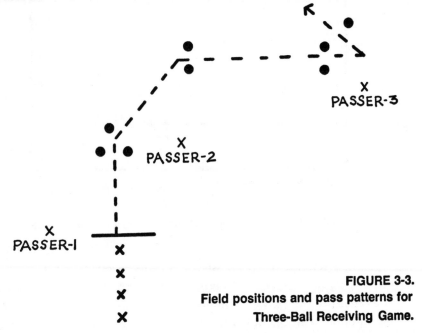

FIGURE 3-3.
Field positions and pass patterns for
Three-Ball Receiving Game.

Variations:

1. Change the pass patterns.
2. Require catches with one hand.
3. Have two stations with teams competing to see who can complete the most passes in a designated amount of time.

QUICK PASS

Object: To be the first team to have each member pass the football to all teammates and successfully shoot a basket.

Equipment: Footballs.

Description:

This game is played indoors on a basketball court. (The game can also be modified and played outside.) Two teams are formed. Each team distributes its players evenly from endline to endline on opposite sidelines. One player from each team has a football and starts passing to teammates on a signal from the instructor.

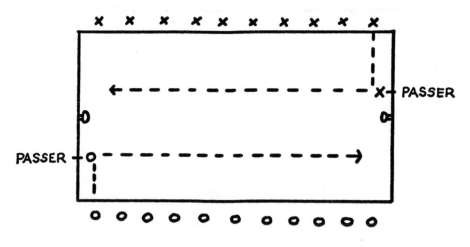

FIGURE 3-4. Player positions and rotation for Quick Pass

After passing to each player on the sideline while moving down the floor, the passer takes the football and shoots a basket. After making the basket, the passer passes to the nearest player on the sideline who becomes the passer. The first passer runs to the endline and everybody moves up one position on the sideline as the passing begins. Teams start passing from the same end of the court each time. The first team having all its players score a basket is the winner.

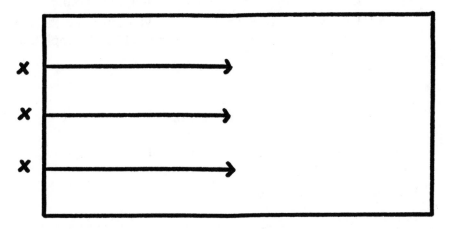

FIGURE 3-5. Starting position for Three-Player Pass game

Variation:
Have the passers stand near the center circle and not move down the court. A new passer comes out when every team member has received and returned a pass.

THREE-PLAYER PASS

Object: To successfully pass the football back and forth while traveling the predetermined distance.

Equipment: Footballs.

Description:
Three players line up on one endline and proceed to pass the ball back and forth until they reach the far endline. They then turn around and pass to each other while returning to the starting point. Players may not run with the ball, and any time the ball is dropped, they must return to the endline where they started. Use several fields at the same time. Each team gets a point every time it passes over the endline.

Variations:

1. Use a basketball weave with the football.
2. Use two or three defensive players.
3. Have a goal to throw at when crossing the endline.
4. Have two teams compete to see who can score the most goals by passing the ball down the field and completing a pass across the endline.
5. Use basketball rules.

FLEETBALL

Object: To practice handling the football and also passing and catching.

Equipment: Footballs and cones.

Description:

The game begins with the players exchanging handoffs on a timed basis. (Figure 3-6.) The players then move to the next phase of the game, which consists of passing, receiving and running a zigzag pattern with the ball. The runner returns and becomes the passer. (Figure 3-7.) Different pass patterns can be required. It is best to have six to eight players on each team so there will be very little standing around. The game is played on a timed basis and the team with the most successful ball exchanges (handoffs and passes) is the winner.

Variation:

Incorporate other football skill drills into the game.

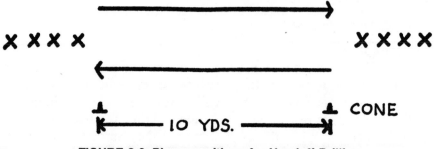

FIGURE 3-6. Player positions for Handoff Drilling

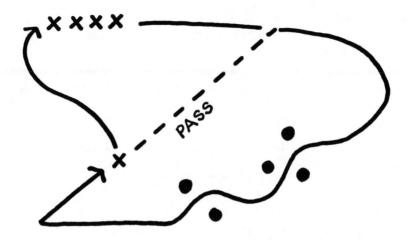

FIGURE 3-7. Passer and receiver positions and sample pass patterns

PUNT OFF

Object: To score points by kicking the ball over your opponent's goal line and having it land on the ground before it is caught.

Equipment: Football.

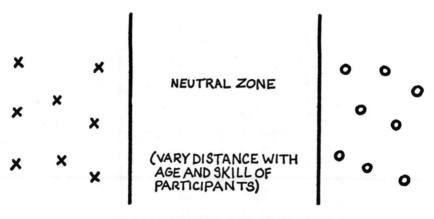

NEUTRAL ZONE

(VARY DISTANCE WITH AGE AND SKILL OF PARTICIPANTS)

FIGURE 3-8. Players' area for Punt Off

Description:

When a ball is caught behind the goal line, the receiving team can punt from their goal line. A ball caught in the neutral zone can be punted from the point of the catch. Players alternate punting from their goal line but the person catching a punt in the neutral zone punts the ball immediately.

Variations:

Use place kicking or passing instead of punting.

KICK FOOTBALL

Object: To punt the ball over the goal line.

Equipment: One football.

Description:

Five players from each team line up in a twenty-yard area. The game starts with one team punting from its own forty-yard line. A member of the opposing team catches the ball and punts it back. Players must stay within their own areas and call for the ball when catching it. If the ball is dropped or missed, the player responsible must take a twenty-yard penalty before punting. When the ball goes over the goal line, one point is scored by the team that kicked the ball.

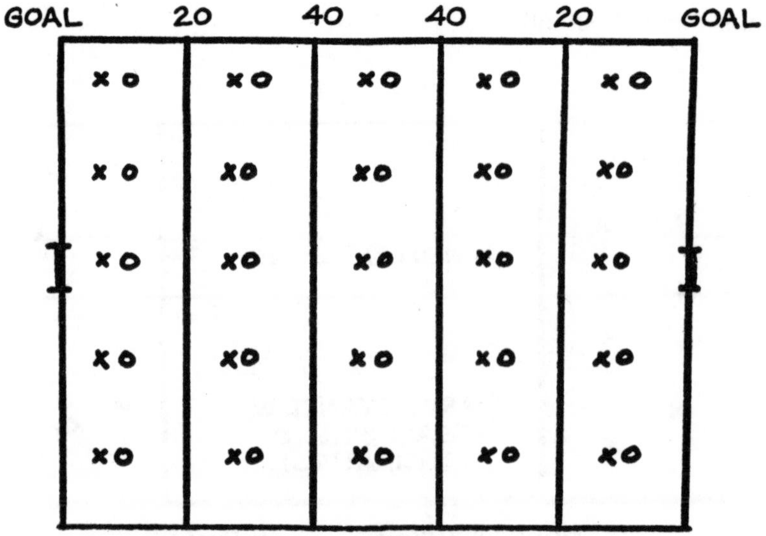

FIGURE 3-9. Player positions for Kick Football

BASKETBALL

MONSTER BALL

Object: To shoot as many lay-ups as possible while the opposing team is completing a task.

Equipment: Four basketballs and an Indian club.

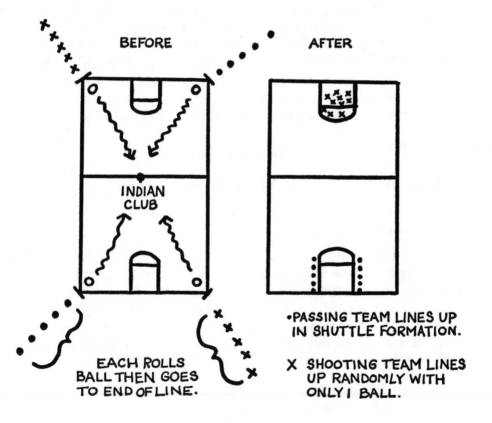

FIGURE 3-10. Player positions before and after the pin is hit

Description:

The class is divided into two teams. Each team is divided in half and the squads face each other diagonally across the gym. (Figure 3-10.) A single Indian club is placed in the center of the gym. Each squad is given a basketball. On the signal, each group rolls its ball trying to knock down the pin. When the pin falls, the team that hit it (both squads) goes to a designated basket in the gym and starts shooting lay-ups. Meanwhile, the other team (both squads) goes to the other end of the gym, lines up in two lines facing each other and begins passing one ball back and forth, up and down the lines until they complete twenty-five (or any number the teacher decides upon) successful passes. The teacher can also decide upon the type of pass to be used. The passing team must count out loud, and when they reach twenty-five, they yell "STOP." The number of lay-ups made during that time with one ball is the number of points scored by the shooting team. All squads then go back to their starting corners in the gym and, on the signal, begin rolling the balls again. No instructions are given to the shooting team except that no one can shoot the ball more than once until everyone on the team has had a chance to shoot. This game provides good practice for lay-ups and passing in basketball.

STATION TASKS

Object: To successfully complete basketball tasks as designated by the teacher.

Equipment: Basketballs and cones.

Description:

Each player is given a task sheet which is to be filled in each day. You can designate the amount of time that is to be spent at each station. The activities at each station are explained and practiced before the students begin their tasks.

Examples of tasks that would be located at stations placed around the gymnasium are:

1. Shooting lay-ups
2. Dribbling around cones

3. Foul shots

4. Wall passes

5. Jump shots

Each student records the number of successful repetitions on the task sheet each day. At the end of the basketball unit, novelty awards can be presented to the students with the best records.

Variations:

1. Students can work on their skills as soon as they come to class instead of standing around waiting for class to begin.

2. Designate the number of repetitions that are to be completed each day and keep one basketball basket free for half-court play for students who have completed their tasks.

THREE-RING CIRCUS

Object: To provide a competitive scrimmage situation which will motivate the students.

Equipment: Basketball.

Description:

Divide the class into groups of three and have four groups (twelve players) at each basket. Two teams play three-on-three basketball games with the losers taking the ball out following the scoring of each point. The third team observes, and the fourth team runs around the gym. When one team scores three points, the observing team starts scrimmaging the winning team. The losing team starts running and the running team observes in order to be ready to play when three points are scored.

Variations:

1. Have the fourth team practice basketball skills such as dribbling, jumping, or ball handling, instead of running.

2. Have the two competing teams work on rebounds by having one of the observing team members shoot the ball so it bounces off the rim or the backboard.

ONE-ON-ONE-ON-ONE

Object: To practice individual offensive and defensive basketball skills in a competitive situation.

Equipment: Basketball.

Description:
This game is played by three players. One player starts with the ball and is on offense. The other two players are on defense until one of them obtains a rebound. This person then becomes the offensive player. The winning score is eighteen.

Variation:
After stopping a dribble, the defensive player must give the offensive player room to get off a shot.

DRIBBLE STEAL

Object: To steal the opponent's ball while at the same time continuing to dribble.

Equipment: A basketball for each player.

Description:
Each player dribbles a basketball while simultaneously trying to disrupt the dribble of another player. The last person dribbling is the winner.

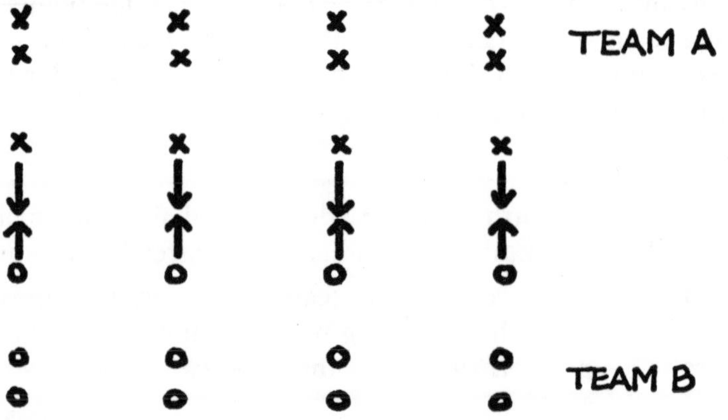

FIGURE 3-11. Formation for playing Dribble Steal on a team basis

Variation:

Make it a team contest by having two teams. The team score is determined by the number of steals after a designated period of time.

WALL REACTION

Object: To catch the ball after the partner throws it against the wall.

Equipment: A basketball for every two players.

Description:

One player lines up facing the wall at a distance of about five to six feet. The other player throws the ball against the wall to make the first player react to catch the ball.

Variation:

Vary the area of the wall that can be hit according to the age and skill of the players.

"21" VARIATION

Object: To be the first player to score twenty-one points by successfully shooting baskets from the point at which the ball was rebounded.

Equipment: Basketballs.

Description:

The shooting proceeds as in a regular game of "21." Each shooter starts with a long shot which is worth two points. The next shot must be attempted from the point where the ball is rebounded. This shot counts for one point. The shooter continues as long as both shots are made.

To put a premium on consistency, a penalty system is followed when both shots are missed. If a player has zero to nine points, the new point total is zero. If the player has ten to twenty points, the new point total becomes ten. When a player misses both shots on consecutive turns, the new total automatically becomes zero.

Variation:

Have two teams competing simultaneously. Two consecutive missed shots by a team will result in point reduction.

THINK PASS

Object: To successfully pass the ball in the manner designated by the instructor.

Equipment: Basketballs.

Description:

Divide the class into groups of five or six and set them in the formation shown in Figure 3-12. The passer alternates passing to each player in the group. The passer starts by using a chest pass. The instructor then calls out a different pass and the passer must alternate using the two passes. The instructor keeps adding passes that must be used in sequence. When a passer uses the wrong pass, another member of the group becomes the passer and the game starts over.

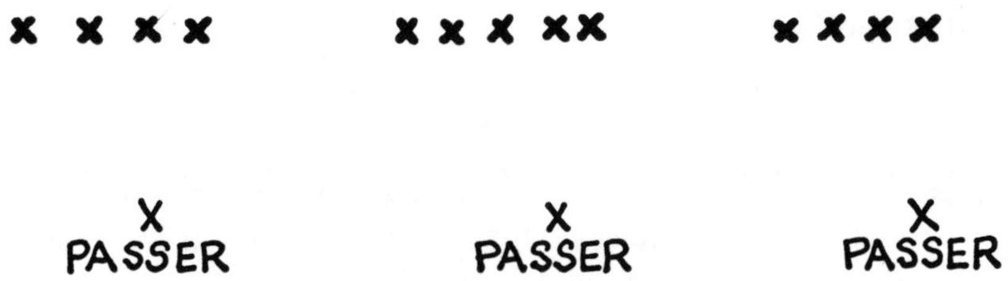

X X X X   X X X XX   X X X X

X   X   X
PASSER   PASSER   PASSER

FIGURE 3-12. Player formation for Think Pass

SOFTBALL

BEANBAG SOFTBALL TOSS

Object: To score as many runs as possible by tossing a bean bag in the scoring zones before striking out.

Equipment: Beanbags.

Description:

Each player throws beanbags at the target until getting three strikes. The number of runs that are scored before striking out becomes the score for the inning. The beanbag is thrown from behind a line which is placed at an appropriate distance from the target area.

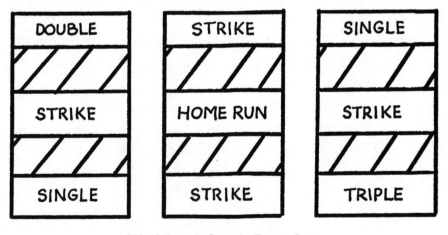

FIGURE 3-13. Sample Target Area

Variations:

1. Small children can throw to see if they can get a hit before landing on a strike.

2. Older children can form teams and play a seven-inning game.

3. The complexity of the target area can be increased for older children.

4. Outs can be used instead of strikes to speed up the action.

DOUBLE PLAY EXCITEMENT

Object: To hit the ball and run as many bases as possible before the fielding team executes a designated double play.

Equipment: Ball and bat.

Description:
One team is at bat and the other team is in the field. After hitting the ball, the batter runs bases until the fielding team is able to execute a short to second to first double play. (For example, if the ball is hit to the centerfielder, the centerfielder must first throw the ball to the shortstop, who will in turn throw the ball to the second baseman who relays the ball to the first baseman.) Every player bats each inning and the winning team is the team with the most total bases.

Variations:

1. Designate different double-play combinations. Pitcher to second to first, first to second to first, etc.

2. Hit the ball off a cone or tee to start play.

3. Use different kinds of balls.

4. Kick the balls instead of hitting them with a bat.

BALL DROP

Object: To emphasize the importance of not throwing the bat after hitting the ball.

Equipment: Bat; softball; bucket.

Description:
The student hitting the ball must place the bat in a bucket before starting to run to first base.

Variations:

Draw a square on the ground where the bat must be placed if a bucket is not available.

SURE-HAND IKE

Object: To teach the players to get the ball in the throwing hand rapidly.

Equipment: Two string rackets with the handles cut off. An elastic band is placed across one side of the racket to hold the racket on the player's fielding hand. (This is an ideal way to make use of broken rackets.)

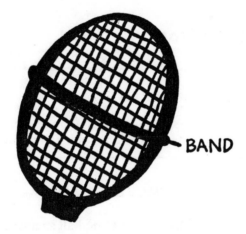

BAND

FIGURE 3-14. Racket with elastic band to keep it on the fielder's hand

Description:

Two lines are formed near a base in a shortstop and second baseman's positions. The first person in each line wears a racket, instead of a glove on his fielding hand. The purpose of the racket is to teach the concept of keeping an open catching hand to allow for a quick release of the ball with the throwing hand to the next base. The instructor rolls the ball to a player in one line. This player traps the ball between the racket and the throwing hand and flips it to the front person in the other line who traps the ball between the

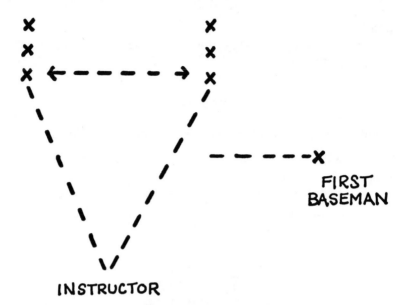

FIGURE 3-15.
Player positions for Sure-Hand Ike

throwing hand and the racket and quickly throws it to the first baseman.

WALL SOFTBALL

Object: To score runs by throwing the ball against the wall in such a manner that the other team cannot field it.

Equipment: Tennis ball; a wall.

Description:
The game is played like softball. The scoring is the same. The batter throws the ball against the wall. After the ball rebounds, the defense must catch the ball before it bounces more than once. If the defender fails to catch the ball, it is either a single, double, triple, or a home run. This depends on the area where it falls. Runs are scored by advancing the players around the bases. The single line is placed approximately ten feet from the wall. Then, depending on the space available, the double, triple, and home-run lines

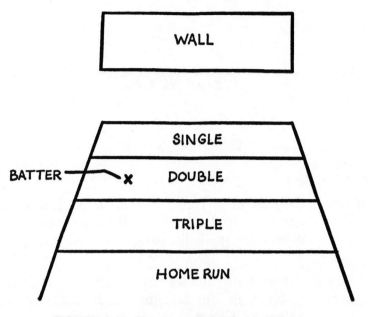

FIGURE 3-16. Diagram of Wall Softball field

are placed accordingly. If the ball hits in front of the single line, it is a strike. The batter is allowed two strikes before being out. If the ball is caught by a defender, the batter is out. Each team is allowed three outs. Any number can play.

FIELD HOCKEY

SHOOTING GALLERY

Object: To practice shooting accuracy.

Equipment: Clothesline; tin coffee cans; three cones; empty plastic detergent or plastic milk bottles; one hockey stick per person; hockey balls; score cards and pencils.

Description:

Set up stations and divide the class into four equal groups with a captain for each group. The captains each have a score card and keep track of their team's score. (Figure 3-17.)

Tie ropes onto the goal cage as shown. Each player will get three tries and will score according to the point values shown. Total the score for each player and enter it on the card. (Figure 3-18.)

	1	**2**	**3**	**4**	
TEAM 1	O-15	O-15	O-9	O-9	GRADE
JOE					
GERT					
TOMMY					
MARY					
JAMIE					

FIGURE 3-17. Team Scorecards

5	4	5
3	2	3
5	1	5

FIGURE 3-18. Station 1

Set up five coffee cans as shown. Each player gets three tries to knock down as many cans as possible. One point is scored per can. A bonus of two points is scored if all three cans in a set are knocked down. (Figure 3-19.)

FIGURE 3-19. Station 2

Attach empty plastic cartons to the goal as shown. One point is scored per goal and two points are scored if the lower carton is hit. Three points are scored if the upper carton is hit. Each player gets three tries. (Figure 3-20.)

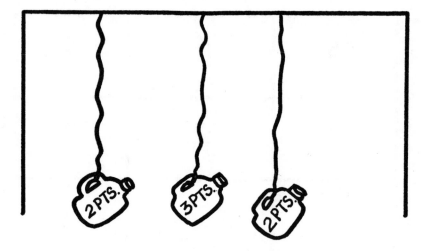

FIGURE 3-20. Station 3

Place cones on their sides and have students stand about five to eight inches away. Have them push pass or drive into the cones. Three points are scored for a goal and one point is scored if the cone is hit with no goal scored. Each player gets three tries. (Figure 3-21.)

FIGURE 3-21. Station 4

GOLF POOL

Object: To get all the balls out of a rectangular area in the least number of hits.

Equipment: Seven hockey balls, one painted or marked with tape; folded mats or boards placed to form a rectangle with each corner open wide enough to allow a ball to pass through it; one hockey stick per player.

Description:

Balls are set up as shown with one ball designated as the cue ball. Using the hockey stick, the first player "breaks" and then hits all the other balls out through the openings. The player with the lowest number of strokes after the designated number of rounds is the winner.

The balls are putted out and the cue ball is hit out last. If the cue ball is hit out before the rest of the balls, there is a five-stroke penalty.

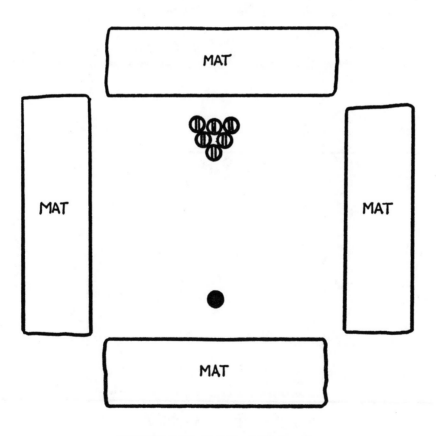

FIGURE 3-22. Golf Pool Rectangle

Variations:

1. One player hits until failing to hit a ball out. The opponent then starts hitting. The winner is the player who hits out the most balls during the game.

2. Play doubles.

3. Number the balls and play rotation pool.

4. Use the cue ball to hit out other balls.

LINE LIFT

Object: To quickly and accurately dribble, pass, and scoop.

Equipment: Two trash cans or boxes; one hockey stick per person; two hockey balls; two hoops.

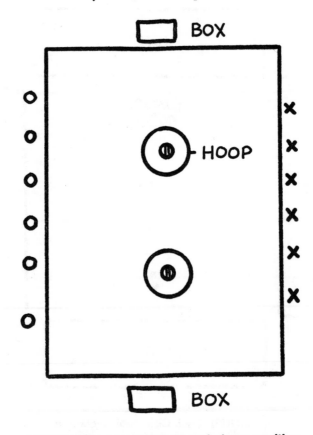

FIGURE 3-23. Line Lift field and player position

Description:

Divide the class into two equal teams and give each player a number. Place trash cans at the ends of the playing area and place balls in the hoops in the center of the field. When a number is called, the players with that number come out to their balls, place them outside the hoop, push pass to three people on their team (the ball must be stopped and controlled by each person before passing), then dribble to the trash can or box and scoop one time trying to get a "goal." They then pick up the ball, run back to the hoop and place the ball in the hoop, and return to their lines. Scoring is as follows:

> three points–successful scoop; first back in line.
> two points–successful scoop only.
> one point–first back only.

DRIVE 'EM CRAZY

Object: To drive the ball as far as possible without raising a stick above the waist, and to dribble quickly.

Equipment: Hockey balls and hockey sticks.

Description:

The class is divided into two teams per game. Each player drives the ball as far as possible, runs down and retrieves the opponent's ball, and dribbles that ball back. The first person back gets a point for his team.

SOOPER SCOOPER

Object: To accurately scoop the balls into the boxes and to be the first team to score twenty points.

Equipment: Empty boxes (with points painted on the sides—optional); eight to ten cones; equal number of balls for each team; one hockey stick per person.

Description:

Set the boxes up in the field with the farthest boxes having the highest point value. The first person on each team is asked to

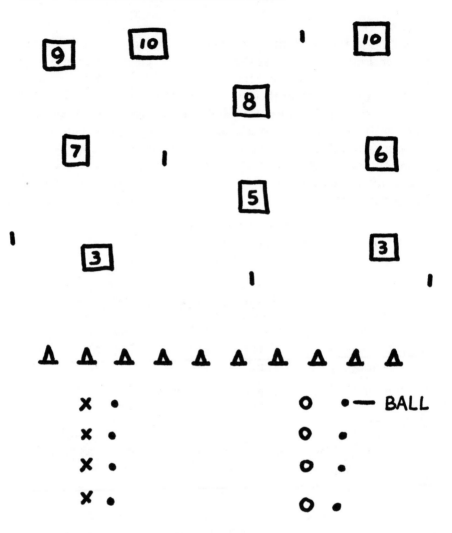

FIGURE 3-24. Cone and box positions for Sooper Scooper

perform one scoop, and if it lands in a box, the team receives those points. If it goes over the cones into the playing area, one point is scored. Both teams continue in turn until twenty points are reached. The balls are retrieved when all the balls have been hit.

QUICK-PASS

Object: To accumulate the highest possible score by completing the greatest number of accurate push passes in the designated time limit.

Equipment: One hockey stick per person; one hockey ball per couple.

Description:

Form two lines five to ten feet apart facing one another, so that each player has a partner standing opposite him. On the signal, partners hit to each other and count the total number of passes between them. (*Note:* The ball must be stopped and controlled before passing.) After fifteen to twenty seconds, shift one line by having the end player move to the front. Repeat play with each player counting his personal score and adding it to his previous score. This continues until each player has passed to every player on the other team. The player with the highest personal score is the winner.

Variations:

Use scoop, drive, flick, emphasizing control between each pass.

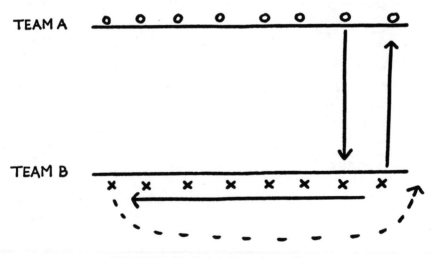

FIGURE 3-25. Quick-Pass formation

MAZE DRIBBLE

Object: To accurately and quickly dribble through the maze without allowing the ball to touch any objects in the maze.

Equipment: Four ropes; five cones; eight hoops; two fold-up mats; four empty boxes; two tires.

Description:

Set up the maze as shown. Players dribble through the maze, one after another, about five feet apart. Each player starts with zero points and must get through the maze without touching boundaries or obstacles along the way. If the ball leaves the maze, add two points and put the ball back in the maze. If the ball hits a piece of equipment, score one point each time. The player with the lowest score is the winner.

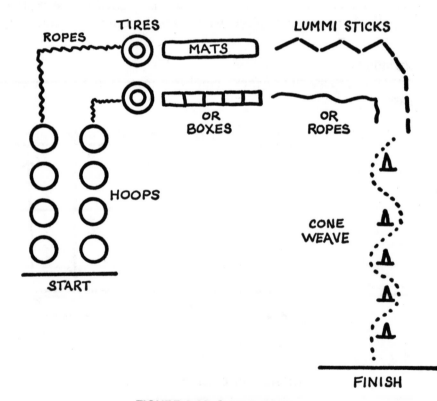

FIGURE 3-26. Sample Maze

VOLLEYBALL

KNEE VOLLEYBALL

Object: To emphasize correct position play for volleyball.

Equipment: One volleyball and knee pads for each player.

Description:

Players either wear knee pads or the game is played on a large mat. A net is placed at the height of a tennis net and the players play the game on their knees instead of in a standing position.

Volleyball rules are used when playing knee volleyball except that the serve consists of a two-handed overhead toss and spiking is not permitted.

Variations:

1. Require two passes before hitting the ball over the net.
2. Mark zones on the floor and have the players play from a standing position without using the spike.

NEWCOMB PROGRESSION

Object: To learn lead-up progressions to volleyball.

Equipment: One volleyball or light plastic ball of volleyball size.

Description:

Start the progression by having the students play newcomb (catching and throwing the ball). The next part of the progression is to require that the first touch after the ball clears the net be a set to a team's member before reverting to newcomb rules. After acquiring success with set newcomb, the players move on to set volleyball which requires a volleyball serve and two sets before the volleyball is returned over the net. The fourth phase requires the second person to set and the third to spike. The first person can catch the ball and throw it to the setter. The fifth part of the progression is to play volleyball with a pass, set, and spike required.

Order of Progression:

1. Newcomb
2. Set Newcomb
3. Set Volleyball
4. Spike Volleyball
5. Volleyball

Variations:

1. Require the second or third person to use the set in either set newcomb or set volleyball.
2. Gradually decrease the amount of time that the ball may be held.
3. Lower the net.

CIRCLE VOLLEYBALL

Object: To learn volleyball skills.

Equipment: Volleyballs.

Description:

On a gymnasium floor, tape two circles, the larger one thirty feet in diameter, and the smaller one six feet in diameter. Two teams take turns in playing an offensive and a defensive game. The team playing offense sends a center player into the small circle and team members scattered around the outside of the larger circle attempt to bat a volleyball over the heads of the opposing players (who are all stationed in the area between the boundaries of the two circles), to their center player. Defensive players intercept passes to the center player by batting the ball.

The ball must be batted with the fingers or a closed hand. It cannot be caught and thrown by any player except the center player. Offensive players cannot step inside or on the line of the large circle; defensive players cannot step outside the large circle. The center player must keep at least one foot inside the small circle. The defensive players cannot step inside the small circle, or on the lines defining these circles. If a ball is caught by any player other than the center player, it is given to the center player, who tosses it to a teammate. If a line violation occurs, the ball is dead and is put into play as at the start of the game.

The game is started by an offensive player who tosses the ball and then bats it to a teammate. The ball cannot be played to the center person after a toss until a player other than the tosser plays the ball.

One point is awarded to the offensive team for a line violation committed by the defensive team. Two points are awarded to the offensive team when the center player gains possession of the ball. Play is continuous, and the center player, after scoring, tosses the ball to a teammate. This toss, as well as the toss after a caught ball violation, cannot be intercepted by an opponent. The game is played for six or more two-minute periods as each team plays offense in alternate periods. The team with the higher score at the end of the playing time wins the game.

Three or four games can be played at one time to involve many students.

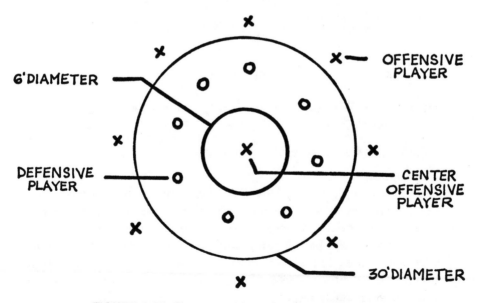

FIGURE 3-27. Player positions for Circle Volleyball

BALL PROGRESSION

Object: To learn volleyball skills by using different kinds of balls.

Equipment: Volleyball; balloon; beachball; plastic ball.

Description:
An exciting way to teach young children the skills of volleyball is to vary the kind of ball that is to be used.

1. *Volleyball* – Start by playing newcomb and use a regular volleyball.
2. *Heavy Balloon* – The students use a heavy balloon to get the concept of a volleyball game.
3. *Beachball* – The beachball is heavier and demands quicker reactions from the players. They continue to develop and improve their understanding and skills.
4. *Heavy Plastic Ball* – This ball is somewhat lighter than a volleyball, but it is possible to closely simulate a volleyball game.
5. *Volleyball* – Students are now ready to again use a volleyball. This time they play regular volleyball because they understand the concepts and rules and have developed the skills needed for volleyball.

BALL OF FIRE

Object: To volley and catch accurately and quickly in order to avoid being caught with the "ball of fire."

Equipment: One volleyball per team.

Description:
Stand in a circle, at least five feet from any other player. The ball is volleyed, using the set pass, to any other player on the circle. This person must catch the ball and then volley to another player and so on. As the ball is being volleyed and caught, the instructor blows a whistle. The player who is in possession of the ball must sit down in the center of the circle while the others continue to volley, until one person remains.

Variations:

1. For younger players, use beachballs, foam rubber balls, etc.
2. Use throwing and catching rather than volleying.
3. Use the bump rather than the set.
4. Use two or more fire balls in each circle.

UP 'N AT 'EM

Object: To develop serving accuracy.

Equipment: One volleyball per team.

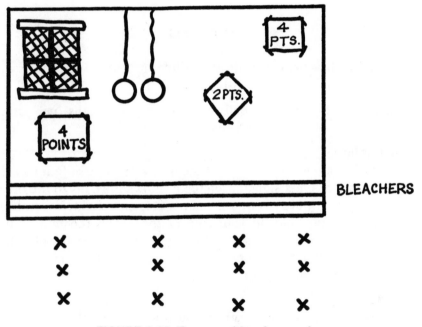

FIGURE 3-28. Team position for serving

Description:

Each team is given one volleyball and is lined up facing a gymnasium wall at a predetermined distance. After instruction has been given on serving, designate target spots on the wall and assess each target a point value (i.e., above the window height and between the rings and the sidewall is worth two points; from the bleachers to the window is worth one point). Actual targets can be taped to the wall at a height above net level.

On a signal, the first member of each team serves at the targets. If the target is hit, that team gets the points. After one score, the ball is given to the next player. Each player continues in turn until the cumulative team points total twenty-one or until the time limit is up.

Variation:

Each line has a different set of targets. Lines rotate to each area until all members score one time at each area. Total the points and compare scores with other teams.

ODD BALL

Object: To have as few balls as possible in your team's possession when the whistle is blown.

Equipment: Seven volleyballs (or other types of balls) per game; nets and standards.

Description:

One team is on each side of the net, with three or four balls in its possession. On a signal, each team throws the balls to the other team, and continues to do so as soon as they are caught. You want as few balls as possible on your side of the net at the end of the designated amount of time. One point is given for each ball in the team's possession at the end of the game, and the team with the lowest score is the winner.

Variation:

Set, serve, or bump rather than throw and catch.

CRISSCROSS

Object: To prevent the volleyball from landing in bounds on your court.

Equipment: Five volleyball standards; four volleyball nets; one or more volleyballs.

Description:

After setting up nets as shown, place four equal teams on each of the four courts. Using either volleyball or newcomb skills, the ball is passed to any other court in an attempt to land the ball on the court of another team. The opposing teams try to prevent this by catching the balls and passing them to other courts. Whenever a ball lands in bounds on a court, that court receives a point. The team with the lowest score wins.

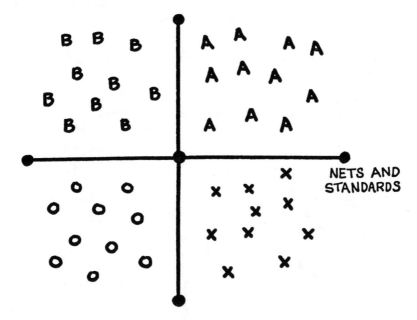

FIGURE 3-29. Court and net positions for Crisscross

Variations:

1. Use more than one ball.
2. Cover the nets with sheets and play a "blind" version.
3. Use a large cage ball that must be volleyed rather than caught.

SET BACK

Object: To practice accuracy in the behind-the-head set.

Equipment: One volleyball per team.

Description:

Players line up one behind the other about five feet apart. The first person throws the ball up and sets it over his or her head to the next person in line who catches the ball and does the same. When it reaches the last person, that person runs to the front of the line and starts again. The game ends when players reach their starting positions. The first team to finish wins.

Variation:

As a challenge, have students try to continue to set rather than catch the ball.

FIGURE 3-30. Player positions for Set Back

SERVE 'EM UP

Object: To practice the skill of serving while learning the proper volleyball rotation.

Equipment: Volleyball net and standards; one volleyball per team.

Description:

Place students on teams in regular volleyball formation. The game is played similar to newcomb but rather than throwing and catching, the ball is served and caught. Each time a player catches the ball, the ball is served from that spot. Any time the ball hits the floor in bounds it is a point against the team whose court it hit. Whenever a whistle is blown, both teams must immediately rotate and continue play. The team with the lowest score is the winner.

Variations:

Use set and catch or bump and catch.

TENNIS

NO RACKET TENNIS

Object: To learn proper court positioning for serving and receiving, as well as scoring methods.

Equipment: One ball; tennis court (or marked area); net and standards.

Description:

Play tennis without using rackets. Players use an underhand hit to serve the ball over the net. Receiving players catch the ball and toss it back underhanded in an attempt to score points. Emphasize proper positioning and score keeping. Players should announce the score clearly.

Variation:

Play doubles, emphasizing court positioning, scoring, and rotation of serve.

FOREHAND "40"

Object: To practice accuracy in tennis skills while being the first team to score forty points.

Equipment: Two tennis balls per game; one racket per line (or per person); tennis nets and standards.

Description:

Divide the class into three equal teams per game. Each team is lined up as shown in Figure 3-31, with two teams playing and one team retrieving the tennis balls. One player per team performs a forehand stroke and scores points according to where the ball lands in the opposite court. If the ball goes out of bounds or into the net, zero is scored. Each player in turn does a forehand stroke until a score of forty is reached, at which time the teams rotate.

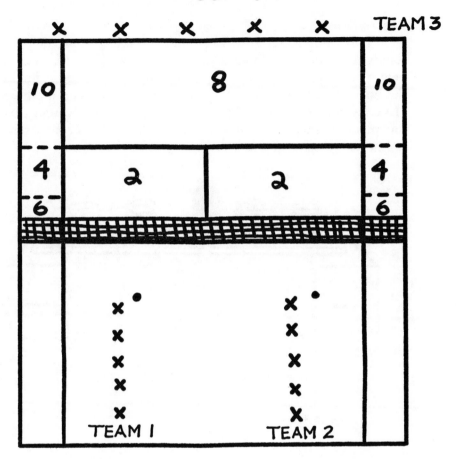

FIGURE 3-31. Court values for playing Forehand "40"

Variations:

1. Use backhand and other strokes.
2. Have players return the throws of retrievers.

TENNIS TARGETS

Object: To accurately serve the ball and knock down targets placed at net height.

Equipment: A long board and empty coffee cans or milk cartons.

Description:

This game is designed to stimulate interest in practicing the tennis serve indoors. Place a board (2″ × 4″, 1″ × 6″, etc.) the height of the tennis net in the gym. (Chairs can be used to hold up the board.) Place empty coffee cans or milk cartons on the board. Have the servers stand in different serving locations behind a base line painted or taped on the gymnasium floor. The servers attempt to knock the cans off the board.

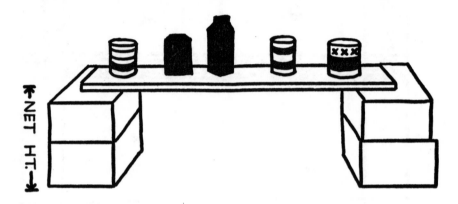

BASELINE

FIGURE 3-32. Set-up for practicing Tennis serves

Variation:

The forehand and backhand strokes can also be practiced with the same targets.

TENNIS TOSS

Object: To make the class aware of the great importance that the toss has to a successful serve in tennis.

Equipment: A tennis ball for each student; a tennis racket for each student.

Description:
The instructor emphasizes that the serve is important. Students are told to each take a ball, find a line on the gym floor which simulates the base line, and find the solution to the following questions:

1. What effect does the height of the toss have on the overall serve?
2. How far from the server should the toss be?
3. What effect does any spin on the ball have on the toss?
4. At what point in the toss should the ball be released from the hand?

When the students feel that they have the answers to the problem questions, they each take a racket, find a spot on the gym floor where they can swing the racket without hitting anyone else, and serve the ball against the wall. They are to experiment and find out whether their assumptions and conclusions regarding the toss are correct or incorrect. Then, they reconvene with their teacher and discuss their solutions as a group.

This teaching style is adaptable to individualized work by the student as well as group examination of the problem.

4

Ready, Set, Go!

38 New and Modified Relay Races

The relay is an excellent way to challenge your students. One of the delightful characteristics of the relay is that it can be designed for a wide range of ages and abilities. We have provided relays for many different skill levels. However, if you would like to use the idea found in a difficult relay for younger children, change the distance, reduce the emphasis on speed, alter the skill demand and/or decrease the competitive aspects. Relays can pep up any of your classes. Think of the relay as a learning tool, an enjoyable activity, a motivator, or a technique to foster cooperation with other students. Relays serve all of these purposes.

Outcomes: Relays are great for learning skills that are being covered in class. We provide examples of relays that can be used with many different activities and supply a framework that will allow you to develop other relays patterned after ours. Your children will be challenged and motivated by relays. We include some that are highly vigorous in nature and others that are relatively slow-paced. You can select the type of relay that best fits into your lesson plan. You will find that our relays encourage a spirit of cooperation and interaction with different members of the class.

Complexity: Basic movement patterns and fundamental skills are included in relays for young children in this chapter. You will find some relays that can be used for any age group simply by varying the distance, the locomotor movement or the equipment. Others incorporate highly skilled movements and are designed for the student with a high degree of coordination and dexterity.

Organization: You can use these relays as part of your regular lesson. For example, in a soccer unit you can use soccer relays as one phase of your drilling for the sport. You can also develop mini games using the sport skills and set these up in the form of relays. An example would be a two-person pass and lay-up relay in a basketball unit. Another way for you to use relays would be to insert a relay or two in the middle of the class period when the students need to be "picked up." Relays can also be used at the beginning and at the end of the class period. They will help you start and/or end your class on a high note.

Formations: There are many different formations that can be used with relays. We suggest that you use a variety of formations to add another dimension of interest to your relays.

Competitiveness: The element of competition is present in all relays. However, many of the relays that we present place emphasis on fun, teamwork and each child's personal satisfaction with his or her own performance rather than on an intense concern over winning. Keep in mind that each child can be a winner in a relay.

Relays provide a great answer for you to give to the question, "What are we doing in Gym today?"

RAPID

RADIAL RELAY

Object: To squeeze through the tire and return quickly to tag the next person in line.

Equipment: One tire per line.

Description:

Form single-line squads. On the signal, run to the tire, pick it up over your head, squeeze your body through it, run to the line, and tag the next person.

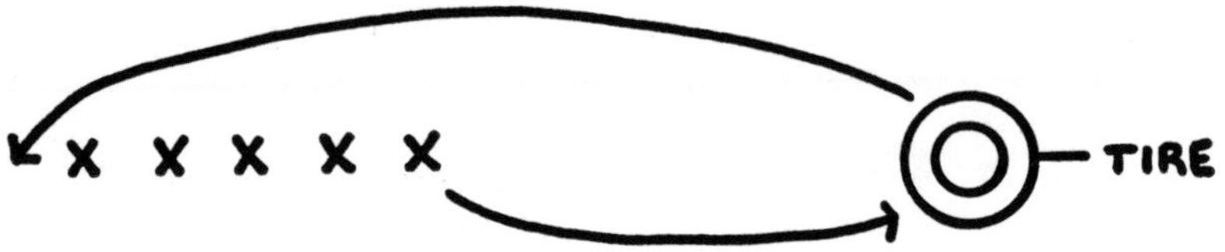

FIGURE 4-1. Radial Relay Formation

REBOUND RELAY

Object: To dribble to the line, chest pass against the wall and quickly return to the starting point.

Equipment: One basketball per line; tape.

Description:

Single-line squads are used. Tape targets on the wall opposite the squads (approximately one-foot square). The first person dribbles up to the designated distance from the wall, chest passes five times at the target, then dribbles to the next person in line. If the ball misses the target, the person must continue until five passes enter the square.

Variations:

Change the type of pass or the distance from the wall.

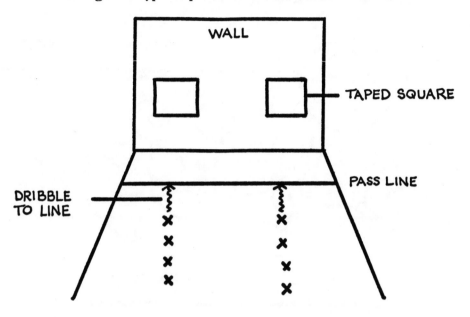

FIGURE 4-2. Player postions for Rebound Relay

PLANET PASS

Object: To pass the cage ball down the line faster than the other teams.

Equipment: One cage ball per line.

Description:

Have students lie down on the floor in a single line with their feet at the shoulder-level of the person in front of them. Then ask them to sit up, legs slightly astraddle. On the signal, the first person lays back, passing the ball to the person behind him and remains lying down. When the ball reaches the last person, she must touch the floor behind her with the ball, then sit up passing the ball forward with each person in turn sitting up and passing. The first line to have the ball reach the front is the winner. There can be ten to fifteen students in a line.

SITTING UP WHILE PASSING

LYING DOWN WHILE PASSING

FIGURE 4-3. Formation for Planet Pass Relay

BALL CONTROL RELAY

Object: To control the basketball while using either the right or the left hand.

Equipment: One basketball for each team.

Description:
The first student of each team must dribble the basketball right-handed while walking from the starting point to the turn-around point. At the turnaround point, the student turns and runs back to the starting point while dribbling left-handed. When reaching the starting point, the student stops, pivots, and *hands* the basketball to the next member of the team. Players may not pass the ball.

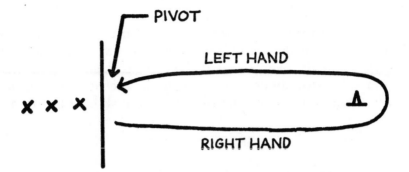

FIGURE 4-4. Route to follow for Ball Control Relay

Variations:

1. Use different pivots.
2. Use only the nondominant hand.
3. Use traffic cones to establish obstacles when dribbling.

TIRE ROLL

Object: To roll the tire to a designated point more quickly than the other teams.

Equipment: One tire per squad; two cones per squad.

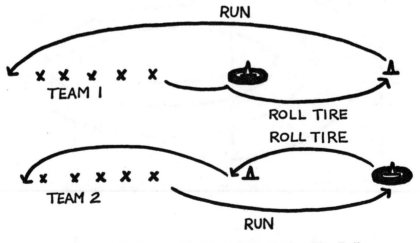

FIGURE 4-5. Route followed when playing Tire Roll

Description:

Have each squad start with a tire over the closest cone. The first person takes the tire off the cone, rolls it to the second cone and places the tire over that cone, then runs back and tags the next person. The second person runs out to the second cone and rolls the tire back to the first cone and so on until all have had turns.

SPACE SHUTTLE

Object: To hook arms with the other team members and reach a designated point sooner than the other teams.

Equipment: None.

Description:

Form shuttle lines of approximately six to eight people. On a signal, Number 1 runs to Number 2 and hooks arms at the elbows. Then Numbers 1 and 2 run to Number 3 and all three hook arms, etc. until all members are hooked in a chain. When all are hooked, one end person must tag a designated area (wall, bleachers, etc.) keeping all hooked, then return to the starting line and be seated. If the team breaks apart, it is disqualified.

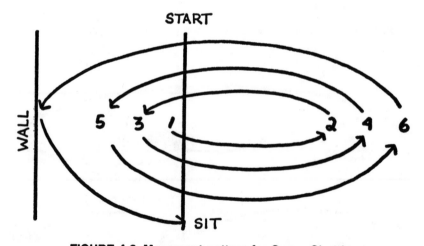

FIGURE 4-6. Movement pattern for Space Shuttle

FOOT-HAND DRIBBLE

Object: To foot- and hand-dribble to the hoops more quickly than the other lines.

Equipment: One soccer ball per line; two hula hoops per line; one basketball per line.

Description:

Set up with squads in a single line. The first player in each squad takes a basketball from the hoop, dribbles it to the second hoop, places it in that hoop, takes out the soccer ball and foot-dribbles to the next person. This person foot-dribbles the soccer ball to the hoop, places it in the hoop and then hand-dribbles the basketball to the line. This continues until all players have had a predetermined number of turns.

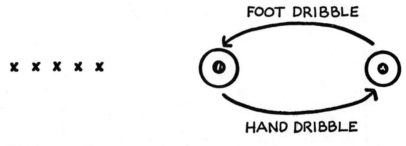

FOOT DRIBBLE

HAND DRIBBLE

FIGURE 4-7. Player positions and movement when playing Foot-Hand Dribble

COMPLEX

BASKETBALL CONE RELAY

Object: To dribble, shoot a lay-up, and return to the line faster than the opponent.

Equipment: Six cones and two basketballs for each basketball court that is used.

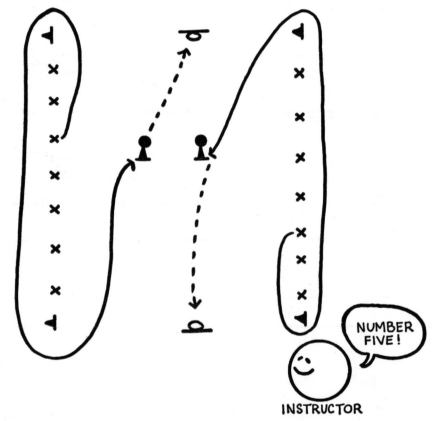

FIGURE 4-8. Team position and traffic pattern for Basketball Cone Relay

Description:

Two teams take their positions sitting between the cones on each basketball court. All the players receive numbers. In the middle of the court are two cones side by side, with a basketball placed on each. The instructor calls a number and the two players with that number stand up, run out, and get their team's ball. They then dribble to their team's basket, make a lay-up, retrieve the ball, dribble back, and balance the ball on the cone. The first person back to his team receives a team point. The instructor then calls another number.

Variations:

1. Use different shots to make the basket.
2. Dribble with the nondominant hand.
3. Incorporate a pass exchange with a stationary teammate.
4. Dribble to the basket, attempt any type of shot (one attempt), retrieve the ball, dribble back to the cone. Points are awarded as follows: One–first done; two–basket made; three–basket made and first done.

WIDE WORLD OF SPORTS

Object: To complete the obstacle course more quickly than the opponents.

Equipment: Four cones; two basketballs; two boxes, two hurdles, two mats, two scooters.

Description:

Form teams equal to the number of baskets that are available. On a signal, the first player on each team runs to the cone, does five jumping jacks, runs to the basket, takes the ball out of the box and takes up to three shots to make a basket (go on after basket is made or after three unsuccessful tries), places the ball back in the box, jumps over the hurdle, does a forward roll, rides the scooter (on his stomach) around the cone and replaces it at the end of the mat, then tags the next person.

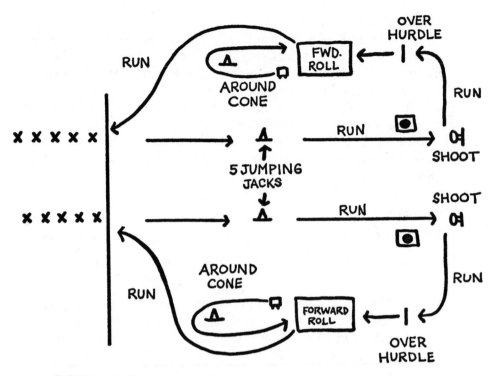

FIGURE 4-9. Diagram of path to follow when playing Wide World of Sports

TUMBLING-HOOP-LA-LA RELAY

Object: To complete the designated tasks more quickly than the other teams.

Equipment: For each team: Tumbling mat, traffic cone, beanbag, hoop hanging from the wall.

Description:

Have each team line up single file. This relay uses tumbling, running, and throwing skills. It is ideal for you to use as part of a tumbling unit. The lead student in each file sprints from the starting point to the tumbling mat. They can perform *any* tumbling skill that they have learned in class. After performing the tumbling activity, they sprint to the beanbag which has been placed about fifteen feet from the wall. They then pick up the beanbag and throw it at a hoop which has been hung on the wall. The students then pick up the beanbag, return it to its place behind the cone, and sprint back to the mat where they do another tumbling stunt of their choosing. They then return to their line and the next person takes a turn.

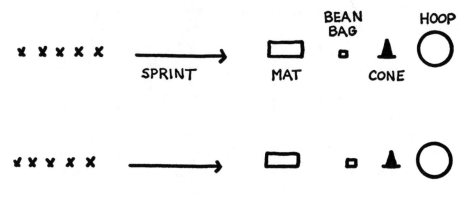

FIGURE 4-10. Positioning of equipment for Tumbling-Hoop-La-La Relay

Variations:

1. Use specific tumbling skills.
2. Use a ball instead of a beanbag, and bounce it off the wall a designated number of times.

SOFTBALL PITCHING RELAY

Object: To be the first team to score twenty-one points by accurately throwing a softball at the target.

Equipment: A softball target and softball for each team.

Description:

Provide a target for each team and have team members alternate pitching to the diagrammed target. The distance from the target is varied according to the age and ability of the participants. The first team to get twenty-one points is the winner.

Variations:

Use this activity for overhead throwing skills and kicking skills also.

FIGURE 4-11. Softball Target

ALMOST ANYTHING GOES RELAY

Object: To complete the events and accumulate the lowest team total of points.

Equipment: Cylinder, climbing ropes, benches, scooters, rope, traffic cones, playground balls.

Description:

There are four people on each relay team to keep everyone moving. A series of six events is provided for each team to complete. A cumulative score is kept to determine the winner of the relay. Points are awarded on the rank order of finishing each race. One for first, two for second, etc. The lowest score wins.

Event 1: *Log roll.* Each person stands on a cylinder (can be the core on which the wrestling mat is rolled) and the time it takes to roll the cylinder forty feet is recorded.

Event 2: *Cumulative long jump.* The first member of each team does a standing long jump with team members 2, 3 and 4 starting where their teammate finishes. The total distance is recorded.

Event 3: *Rope swing.* Two team members stand on a bench approximately ten feet on either side of the rope. Team member A swings across and hands the rope to team member B, who in turn swings and hands the rope to team member C. The swinging and exchanging rope continues until the team members are back to their starting positions. The fastest time determines the team winner.

Event 4: *Back Seat Driver.* One person sits on a scooter while his or her blindfolded partner pulls him or her through six to eight strategically placed traffic cones. Winners are determined on a time basis with a time penalty for hitting the cones.

Event 5; *Backward Over-the-Head Pass.* Members of each team pair off and stand back to back ten yards apart. At a signal, the team member with the ball throws it backward over his or her head to the partner who is allowed to turn around. After catching the ball, the player must always turn and throw the ball backward over his or her head. The number of catches in a timed period determines the winner.

Event 6: *Obstacle Course.* An obstacle course is arranged using class equipment. Each player is timed when completing the course.

Variation:

The types of events are limitless. Let students determine wild events (providing they are safe).

RESCUE RELAY

Object: To "rescue" the group by carrying them over the "mine" field in the shortest time.

Equipment: Wrestling mat, stop watch, ten to fifteen tires, two cones.

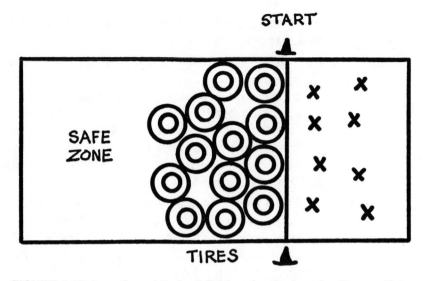

FIGURE 4-12. Location of "mine" field and safe zone for Rescue Relay

Description:

Teams of ten to fifteen are best. Set up tires close together on top of a mat. The group must be transported as quickly as possible over the "mine" field and into the "safe" zone. Only two people per team may touch the mine field at any time and all others must be carried across to safety. If any person, other than the two rescuers, touches the tires, that person must go back to the cones and be transported again. The effort is timed and the team with the lowest time is the winner.

NOVELTY

BOX CAR

Object: For two partners to move the box around the cone more quickly than their opponents.

Equipment: One empty medium-size box per line; one cone per line.

Description:

Players 1 and 2 of each team stand facing forward, one behind the other. A box is placed between the two at waist level. Partners must keep the box between them without using their hands or dropping it, and maneuver around the cone and back. They then hand the box to the next set of partners. If the box falls, they must start over.

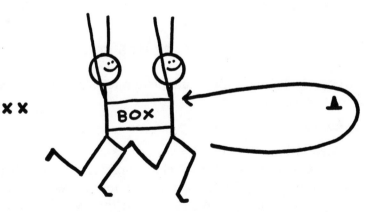

FIGURE 4-13. Player positions when playing Box Car

SPEED SKATING

Object: To "skate" around the cone and back to the line quicker than the other lines.

Equipment: Two shoe boxes per line; one cone per line.

Description:
Place one box on each foot. Shuffle or "skate" around the cone and back to the line. Give the boxes to the next person in line.

FIGURE 4-14.
Speed Skating position

AWARENESS RELAY

Object: To make the students aware of the use of various body parts.

Equipment: Books, papers.

Description:
Pass out one 3" × 5" card to each group member. Each card has a task on it. Students must complete tasks in their numerical order. The first group to finish all the tasks is the winner. Each person completes an assigned task and then touches another member of the team to start the next task.

Task 1 – Open a book to page 73 without using your hands.

Task 2– Pick up a book and carry it to a teammate without using your hands.

Task 3 – Put on your sock with only one hand.

Task 4– Write your name on a piece of paper without using your hands.

Task 5 – Open a door without using your hands.

Task 6 – Tie your shoe without using your thumbs.

Task 7– Make three folds in a sheet of paper without using your hands.

Task 8 – Remove a piece of masking tape with your toes.

Variations:

1. Develop different tasks.

2. Vary the distance to reach the point of carrying out the task.

3. Rotate the cards so each student can be challenged by all the tasks.

EASY DOES IT

Object: To place the ping pong ball on the soda bottle and return to the line as quickly as possible.

Equipment: Two empty one-liter soda containers per line; one ping pong ball per line.

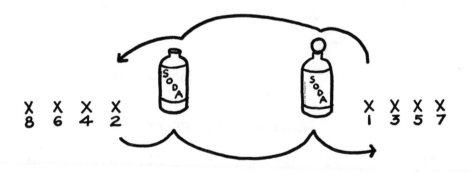

FIGURE 4-15. Team positions for Easy Does It

Description:

Form shuttle lines with each team and line up behind the soda containers placed ten yards apart. Put a ping pong ball on the mouth of one soda container. On a signal, Player 1 runs up to the first container, removes the ping pong ball and places it on the second container, then tags Player 2 who does the same. If the container or ball falls, it must be set up again by the person who tipped it.

CLEAN SWEEP

Object: To sweep the paper pieces across the line more quickly than the opponents.

Equipment: One broom per line; three crushed sheets of newspaper per line.

Description:

On a signal, Player 1 sweeps the pieces of paper across the line, then hands the broom to Player 2, who sweeps the papers back. *Note:* Don't crush paper too tightly or it will be possible to bat it across the line rather than sweep it across.

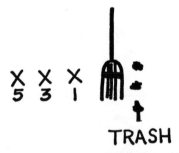

FIGURE 4-16. Player position for Clean Sweep

NUMBER SEARCH RELAY

Object: To collect the numbered cards and place them in sequence more quickly than the opponents.

Equipment: A set of numbered cards for each team.

Description:

The first member of each team runs to a designated location and finds a card with the number 1. The student then returns to the team base, places the number on the floor and tags a teammate who goes to find number 2 and repeat the process. The players pick up numbers until a predetermined number is reached. Numbers are placed in sequence in a designated area behind each team.

Variations:

1. Use letters.
2. Use different locomotor skills when going to the numbers.
3. Mathematics problems can be used.

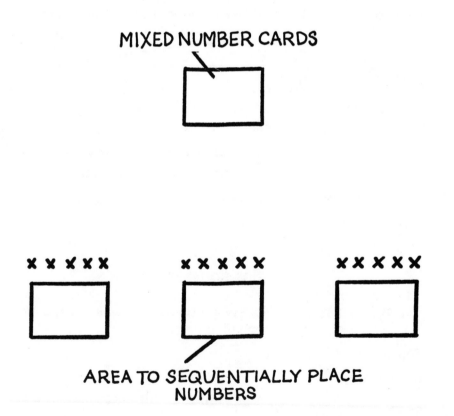

FIGURE 4-17. Team and card location for playing Number Search Relay

OFF TO MARKET

Object: To "go to market" and collect groceries more quickly than the opponents.

Equipment: One empty grocery bag per line; one box per line; five empty food containers per line (examples: egg cartons, soda containers, cereal boxes, etc.); one hat; one coat or shirt per line; one cone per line.

Description:

On a signal, put on the hat and coat and take the grocery bag to the box filled with food containers. *One by one*, place the containers into the bag, run around the cone and back to the box. Empty the bag into the box, run back to the line, take off the hat and coat and give the grocery bag to the next person in line.

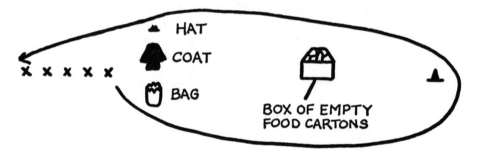

FIGURE 4-18. Floor set-up for playing Off to Market

TIRE SQUEEZE

Object: To squeeze members of a team through a bicycle tire more quickly than the opposing teams.

Equipment: Bicycle tires.

Description:

Two or more circles with an equal number of players are used. Two players clasp hands inside the tire as shown in Figure 4-19.

The tire is passed around the circle without the players letting go of their hands. The team getting its tire back to the starting

FIGURE 4-19. Starting position with the tire

position is the winner. Each player must "squeeze" through the tire as rapidly as possible to move the tire around the circle.

Variations:

1. Use parallel lines and start the tire on the outstretched arm of the player on one end of the line.
2. Use hoops or inner tubes.
3. Require a designated leg to go through the tire first.

BUCKET BRIGADE (Outdoors)

Object: To pass the water bucket to teammates quickly and without spilling its contents.

Equipment: One bucket of water per line (each filled to the same level).

Description:

Form shuttle lines and have the first person carry the bucket, being careful not to spill the water, to the person in the opposite line who carries it back until all have carried it. Award one point for the team with the most water left in the bucket, and one point for the first team to finish.

FIGURE 4-20. Shuttle position for Bucket Brigade

Variations:

1. If indoors, use balls to fill the bucket. If any are dropped, start over.

2. Use a single-line formation and pass the bucket down the line until it reaches the last person, who runs to the front of the line and passes it. Continue this until original positions are reached.

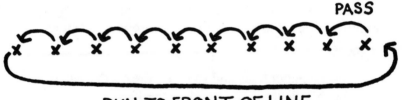

FIGURE 4-21. Single-line formation for Bucket Brigade

ICE CREAM CONE

Object: To carry the ice cream cone around a pin and flip it to the next team member as quickly as possible.

Equipment: One pin per line; one soccer ball or volleyball per line; two small traffic cones per line.

Description:

Players 1 and 2 in each line have cones held upside down. Number 1 places the ball on top of the cone and runs, carrying the cone and ball with both hands held away from the body. Hands may

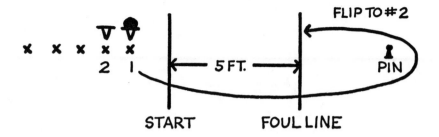

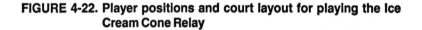

FIGURE 4-22. Player positions and court layout for playing the Ice Cream Cone Relay

not touch the ball. The player runs around the pin and back to the foul line. At this point the ball is flipped to Player 2 who attempts to catch the ball with the cone and then proceeds around the pin. If the ball falls while being caught, pick it up and start from behind the starting line. If it is dropped while running, start over.

5

Help ...
I Can't Breathe!

31 Ways to
Utilize Limited Space

Many teachers are faced with the problem of providing a varied activity program in limited space. We have devoted this chapter to providing you with activities and unique games that will keep your students challenged even though the space is inadequate for games that you might have included in your lesson plans.

Another problem in a cramped space situation is providing sufficient vigorous activity to meet physical needs and release the emotional drive that has been building while your students have been sitting in class. The majority of the games we have included in this chapter are vigorous in nature even though a rather large group of students will be contained in a designated area that is smaller than would be ideal.

Tennis is an extremely popular sport throughout North America and in many other parts of the world. To capitalize on this fact we have included several tennis game modifications. Many times you might like to include a unit on tennis or, for your younger children, a unit designed to develop tennis skills. This is frequently difficult because you have insufficient tennis courts for two or four students per court or you don't have any courts at all. We have designed tennis skill games for you to use either with a limited number of courts or without any courts. Keep in mind that you can modify even the games we diagram on tennis courts to be played on a gymnasium floor or the hard surface portion of your playground.

We would all like to teach under ideal conditions which include unlimited facilities. Most of us never attain this luxury. Therefore, we suggest that you select activities that will provide the same beneficial results your students would receive participating in other activities if you had unlimited space. We have provided games of this type for you in this chapter.

We also encourage you to scan the games and activities in the other chapters in this book. Many of them are also ideal to use where space is limited.

KING/QUEEN OF THE BONGO BONGOS

Object: To become the King or Queen by being the last one to remain in the circle.

Equipment: Wrestling mat or, if outdoors on grass, a designated circle.

Description:

All players must remain on their knees throughout the entire game. Players try to push other players out of the circle, while trying not to be pushed out. The last remaining player is the King or Queen.

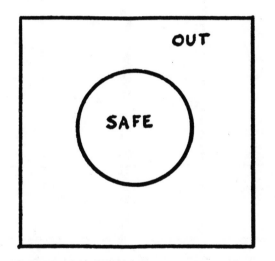

FIGURE 5-1. Playing Area for Bongo Bongos

BOX TENNIS

Object: To learn the basic strokes and scoring of tennis.

Equipment: Gymnasium, utility room, or asphalt area; tennis balls; chalk or tape.

Description:

This game is played according to the rules of tennis, with modifications in serving. Scoring is the same as in tennis. The game is played on a court five feet wide and ten feet long. A center line divides the court into two 5' × 5' courts. A line two feet from the center line on each side marks the service area. A drop serve is used. The hand is used as the racket. Proper forehand and backhand form can be practiced.

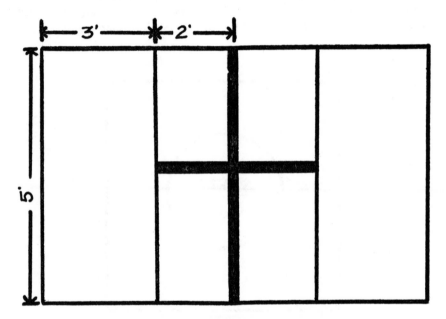

FIGURE 5-2. Court dimensions for Box Tennis

TEAM WALL COUNT

Object: To be the first team to score fifty points.

Equipment: Marked wall and one six-inch playground ball.

Description:

Two to ten players are on a team. Players on each team are numbered consecutively and must hit the ball in sequence. A player can be in the playing area only when hitting the ball. As soon as the ball is hit, the player must run off the court and wait for his next turn. The server must hit Square 1 and the opponent must hit Square 2. The teams alternate hitting the numbers in sequential order until someone misses. The rebound off the wall must land in the boundaries and must be hit on one bounce. If a player fails to hit the next consecutive numbered box or the ball fails to land in bounds, or it bounces more than once, the opposing team receives the point value of the last successful hit. Service changes after each miss.

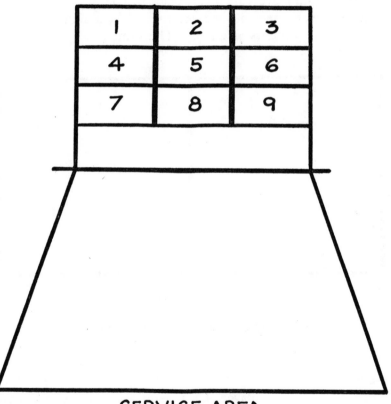

SERVICE AREA

FIGURE 5-3. Team Wall Count markings and court layout

Variations:

1. Let the players hit any number and keep a cumulative score for each team.

2. Make a cooperative game and have the players see how many consecutive numbers they can hit before missing.

ASPHALT TENNIS

Object: To play a table tennis variation on a hard surface.

Equipment: Nets or ropes and standards; paddles and paddle balls.

Description:
Two to four players are on each side of a net which is placed on a hard surface. Dimensions are determined by available space and the number of students on a team. The game is played with table tennis rules.

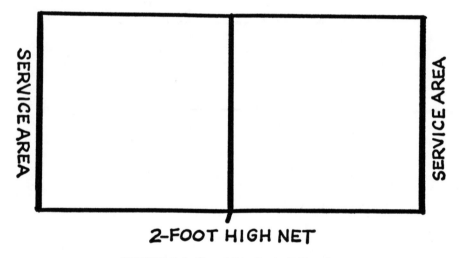

FIGURE 5-4. Court for Asphalt Tennis

Variation:
Play with more players on a team and require two passes before the ball is hit over the net.

GOLF SWING PROGRESSION

Object: To develop a complete golf swing after learning the proper grip, stance, and body position.

Equipment: Three golf clubs of different lengths (for example, a 9 iron, 5 iron and 2 iron); three shoe boxes, one covered with a rug or synthetic turf material; golf balls.

Description:

The student starts with the shortest club and hits the ball off the three stacked shoe boxes. After developing a proper swing with a short club, one box is removed and the longer club is used. Next, the longest club is used with one shoe box. Finally, the full swing is used with the shoe box lid covered with synthetic turf or a rug remnant. Proper fundamentals for the swing and body rotation are emphasized at each phase of the progression. Your students will make faster progress and receive greater self-satisfaction because of the use of the shortened club and the raised ball.

Variation:

If different-length clubs aren't available, start by choking the club and gradually have your students move their hands to the end of the club.

ANGLE HANDBALL

Object: To hit a ball into your opponent's box so it can't be returned to your playing area.

Equipment: Tennis ball, rubber ball, or handball.

Description:

One player starts serving and serves until a point is lost. The ball is bounced for the serve and hit underhand against the wall. The ball must hit the wall and rebound into the opponent's box. Players can score only when serving. Fifteen points determine the winner. The sizes of the boxes depends on skill and space available. Having space between the wall and the boxes will eliminate collisions.

Variations:

1. Play with two or three players alternating hitting the ball from each box area.

2. Require players to hit with the nondominant hand or with both hands.

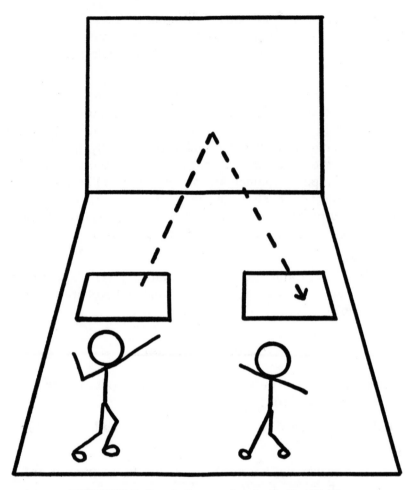

FIGURE 5-5. Court diagram for Angle Handball

3. Older students can use a soccer ball and be required to use their feet when returning the ball to the wall.

TENNIS BALL SHUFFLE

Object: To earn points by finding your team's tennis ball and the special ("S") ball.

Equipment: A tennis ball with a number on it for each team plus a special tennis ball marked with an "S."

Description:

The class is divided into three- or four-person teams. The first person in each line turns and faces his teammates. These players then throw their team's ball over their head into the center of the circle formed by the teams. The teacher simultaneously throws the "S" ball into the circle. The players who threw the tennis balls then turn and try to retrieve their team's ball. If they pick up another team's ball they can throw it up in the air. (If they throw it out of the circle they are disqualified.) When a player finds his team's ball, he runs and hands it to the next person on the team. He can then start searching for the "S" ball. The player finding the "S" ball runs and hands it to the teacher. When the teacher has the "S" ball, the game stops. One point is given to each team that has its team ball in the next player's hand and the team with the "S" ball receives three additional points. The game continues with the next player in each line throwing the ball over his head into the circle.

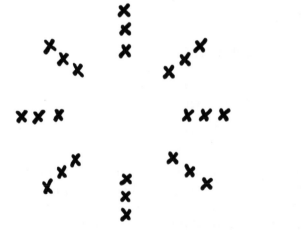

FIGURE 5-6. Player positions for playing Tennis Ball Shuffle

Variations:

1. Permit the players to throw the ball to the next person in line rather than handing it to them.

2. Let the players pick up any ball and get the point total on the ball. The "S" ball could be valued at twenty.

3. Require different forms of locomotion when returning the team's ball to its line.

ROTATION BALL

Object: To hit the ball over the tennis net so that the opposing team cannot return it.

Equipment: One tennis ball per court.

Description:

Four to six players are on each side of a tennis court. A rotation system such as that used in volleyball is followed. The game is started by one player bouncing the ball and striking it, with an open hand, into the opponent's diagonal court. The serve is always made from the right court. The serving distance from the net is determined by the age and skill level of the players. Only one bounce is permitted before the ball is returned over the net. Each player serves for three points and then the serve goes to the other team. Thirty points constitute a game.

TENNIS HUSTLE

Object: To develop skill in the placement of the tennis ball and to provide vigorous physical activity.

Equipment: One tennis ball and four tennis rackets.

Description:

Eight to twelve players line up behind one another on each side of the tennis court on the center mark. Players 1 and 2 and A and B have tennis rackets. Player A puts the tennis ball into play into the tennis court of Player 1. Player A, after hitting the ball, hands the racket to Player C and runs to the other side of the court behind Player 8. Player 1, after hitting the ball successfully over the net, hands the racket to Player 3 and runs to line up behind Player H. Play continues until a player misses the ball. Each miss spells a letter in the word HUSTLE. When players spell HUSTLE, they are out of the game and move to the end of the court to help retrieve missed tennis balls. When all but two players are left on either side of the net, they do not run around to the other court but

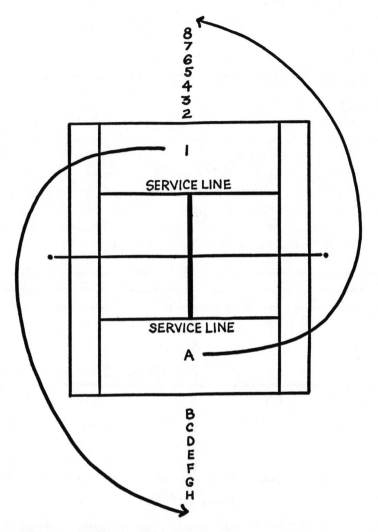

FIGURE 5-7. Player positions on a tennis court for Tennis Hustle

place their rackets on the ground, turn around in place, pick up their rackets and assume a ready position to receive the ball.

Variations:

1. Specify the stroke students can use.
2. Play a game on a team basis with players running to the backs of their own lines after hitting the ball.

TENNIS HANDBALL

Object: To teach racket skills in a limited space.

Equipment: Tennis balls; spray paint.

Description:
Mark tennis courts with dimensions of 9′ × 16½′ on a blacktop area. A playground area or parking area works well. Spray on a dotted line to represent the net.

Have the students start by practicing hitting small playground balls over the "net." They then can play Four Square with a tennis ball. When the students become proficient in controlling the ball, they can play singles and doubles tennis. All games on this court are played by hitting the ball in handball fashion.

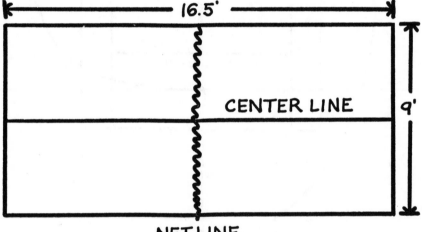

FIGURE 5-8. Modified tennis court for Tennis Handball

Variation:
Increase the number of players on a team and have them alternate hitting the ball.

PITCH-HIT TENNIS

Object: To learn to hit the tennis forehand stroke with accuracy.

Equipment: Tennis ball and racket for each court.

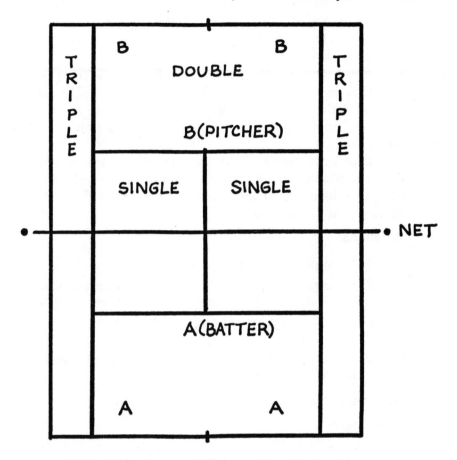

FIGURE 5-9. Player positions for Pitch-Hit Tennis

Description:

Three or four players are on each team. One team is the hitting team and one team is the fielding team. One player on Team A becomes the batter and stands a few feet behind his service court directly opposite and facing the pitcher on Team B who stands on the back edge of the service court on the other side of the net. Players on Team A line up behind the batter and serve as catchers while waiting for their turn to hit. The other players on Team B can position themselves anywhere on their court.

The pitcher throws the ball to the batter to allow a forehand hit with the tennis racket. The fielders try to catch the ball before it bounces within the court. If the ball is caught before it hits the ground, it is an out. It is also an out if the batter hits the ball out-of-bounds or into the net.

Any ball that falls within Team B's service court is ruled a single. A ball landing in the back court is a double and a ball landing in the 4½ foot doubles lane on either side is considered a triple. A ball dropped by a fielder will count as a hit in whichever box it falls.

Each batter bats until making three outs. Runs are counted for each batter and a team total is computed after each player bats. After each batter on Team A has had a turn at bat, Team A goes on defense and Team B bats.

Variations:

1. Have players use the backhand stroke.
2. Have the teams play a seven-inning baseball game.

PROGRESSIVE HANDBALL

Object: To meet the handball challenge of all players and become the ACE (winner).

Equipment: Handball, tennis ball, or playground ball.

Description:

This game is played against a long wall or a surface such as a sliding door partition in a gymnasium. Each player is assigned a section of the wall to protect. (The section can be marked with tape or paint.) If the ball hits a player's section of the partition, that player must return the ball to the wall before it bounces more than once.

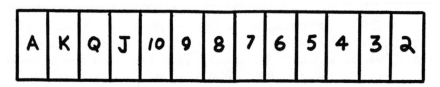

FIGURE 5-10. Wall markings for Progressive Handball

The first player on the left is designated as the ACE, the second the King and so on until each player has a card number. Players must return balls striking their section of the wall. When a player fails to return the ball, he or she drops out of the game and the players move up one space. The last remaining player is the ACE and the winner.

Variations:

1. Have extra players move in to play when a player drops out of the game.

2. The game can be played on a timed basis and the player in the ACE position at the end of the time limit is the winner.

3. Players move to the deuce postion if they fail to return a shot hitting their partition providing there is a playing position for each player.

BIG FOOT

Object: To practice putting skills.

Equipment: Golf balls and putters.

Description:

Have the students line up on the foul lines of a basketball court and face each other. Have each student take off one shoe and walk to the center court line. Have them place their shoes on the floor with the opening facing them. They then go back to the foul line and putt the golf balls into their own shoes. The student with the most balls in his or her shoe at the end of the game is the winner. (The students with large feet have a definite advantage in this game!)

Variations:

1. Vary the distance from the shoes according to the ability of the students.

2. Provide points for hitting the shoe as well as going in the shoe.

3. Use field hockey sticks and balls.

BEACH BALL COOPERATION

Object: To develop cooperative skills in keeping a ball in the air.

Equipment: A tennis racket and a beach ball for each team.

Description:
    This game can be played with three to twelve players forming a circle. The game is started by throwing the beach ball in the air. The person with the tennis racket must hit the ball up in the air and *hand* the racket to another player who will hit the ball next.

    The team receives two points for each time the ball is hit in the air and one point if it is hit on the first bounce.

Variation:
    Require the teams to pass the racket to at least two players before it can be used.

6

I Hope to Get to Bat This Semester!

Over 40 Ideal Games
for Large Classes

Large classes pose a challenging hurdle for every physical educator. Very few of us always have ideal-size classes. Sometimes the class might not be considered exceptionally large in terms of sheer numbers, but a combination of student numbers and the inadequacy of the teaching facility combine to make the class too large in terms of teaching effectiveness. We have included over forty games in this chapter to assist you in making your classes not only manageable but also an enjoyable and challenging learning experience.

A particularly important consideration with large classes is participation. Often, children in a large class spend too much time standing around waiting for their turns or are relegated to inactive roles in the class activity. Our activities emphasize keeping every student active, or moving the action in the class so rapidly that a student should never get bored, even though he isn't always in the mainstream of the activity. The excitement generated by anticipating what is about to occur and preparing to return to the action is a key factor in keeping children enthusiastic throughout a class period even though the class is large.

It should be remembered that simplicity is important when dealing with large classes. Don't use too many different formations so it becomes difficult to move the players. This is important both to get the game started and to keep the action flowing. Also, you will note that we use ingredients of familiar games so the students have a point of reference. A minimum number of verbal directions should be used once the game is explained and the students know the basic rules.

Mass games must never be thought of as simply a way to handle a large class. Think of them in terms of the educational outcomes that the students will receive. In addition to having fun, developing motor and physical fitness, and benefiting from the social interaction that takes place, our games emphasize the development of body mechanic fundamentals. Throwing, kicking, catching, developing agility, refining balance skills and honing coordination techniques are key parts of the games that we have included.

To use these games effectively, you must be prepared. This means that you must know the game thoroughly. It is good to have a trial run with a smaller group if you are unsure of some facets of the game. Have the equipment ready to use when the class starts. This also means that all special floor markings must be completed and boundary cones, game lines, and special equipment must be in place on the playing area.

Have the entire class situated so they can hear you when you explain the game. It is good to use visual aids in your explanations. Don't talk too much when explaining the game. Be concise and let students ask pertinent questions, but try to keep the period of inactivity as short as possible. One of the most important considerations when you have a large class is to get them active as soon as possible. The more students there are, the more chance there is for horseplay.

If possible, have some of the students demonstrate any facets of the game that might be difficult to understand from only a verbal explanation. With small children, every attempt should be made to explain the game by having them get in the formation that will be used. This makes the game much clearer and helps them know where they are to go as the game begins.

The first time you play one of these games you might find that some of your students have misunderstood some of your explanations. Don't hesitate to stop the game and straighten out any problems. You might select some of your more skilled students to be the leaders the first time you play a new game. This will give the other students the advantage of being able to observe some of the more complicated aspects of the game before they are expected to assume a leadership role.

Enter into the excitement of the activity. Show your enthusiasm and interest. Both are contagious.

There are many techniques that can be used to group students in a large class. For the games that require subgroups, experiment with different ways to see which is most effective for you. One good way is to have all the students get in a circle and then designate divisions of the circle to make the appropriate size groups that are needed for the game. These smaller groups can then make other circles to hold the groups until they move into position to play the game. Having the children line up on a line, or get in a circle and number off according to the number of teams that are needed, are other fast and effective techniques to use. Selecting leaders and having students line up behind one of the leaders can also work. However, be sure you rotate your leaders and make certain some children aren't shunted aside because they aren't friends of the leaders.

To get children in the different formations required for the games, they must, of course, understand the concept of scattering or distributing themselves randomly around a designated area. Children with a good movement background usually do not have difficulty. A straight line is easy to form by having your students line up on a line on the playground asphalt or gymnasium floor. To form a double circle, have the students select a partner and get in a circle. One partner then stands in front of the other and the double circle is formed.

Don't hesitate to make modifications in the games. We know that students differ. Sometimes, just a small change or variation will bring out the spark that seems to be lacking. Don't be afraid to listen to your students. Be alert to any comments and observations that they make.

Large classes are not ideal for maximum teaching effectiveness. However, what we are saying in this chapter is don't throw up your hands in disgust and cheat your students. Make use of mass games that will be of value to them and maintain the integrity of your program. A quality program will gain support for physical education and give you assistance in your struggle to get smaller classes. Also, there will be some occasions when it will be necessary to combine classes for a day, or you may have an unforeseen facility conflict, or an assembly that is scheduled. You will suddenly be faced with a large class. On these occasions, use games from this chapter to provide an enjoyable physical education experience.

SINGLE PERIOD ACTIVITIES

CARPET MELEE

Object: To get physiological benefits from sliding around the gymnasium floor.

Equipment: Two small pieces of carpet for each participant.

Description:

The class is divided into two equal teams. One team starts at each end of the gym. On a signal, both teams move to the other end of the gym by sliding on their carpets. Five points are given to the team whose player is first across the finish line. One point is also given for each player who makes it across the finish line. Any player who slips off a carpet must stop at that point, and any player who makes contact with another person (teammate or opponent) is also out of the game.

Variations:

1. Play various games but require the players to use carpet "shoes."
2. Give each team three balls that they must carry to the other end of the floor.
3. Passing or sliding can be used to move the ball.
4. Any player touched while holding the ball must give the ball to the nearest opponent. A dropped ball also goes to the opposing team.
5. Vary the number of balls that each team is given to start the game.

CHECKER HOOPS

Object: To have all the players reach the first row of hoops in their opponent's end of the checkerboard before their opponents can accomplish the same feat at their end.

Equipment: Groups of sixteen hoops or a floor composed of squares of different colors.

Description:

Four teams of four players each play this game. Two players from each team start the game, and when a player reaches a hoop at the far side of their square, another player enters the game. The fourth player starts when a second player reaches a hoop on the far side also. A team wins when all four players have reached the far hoops.

Players move one space on an alternating basis. If a player lands in a hoop with another player, that player must move back to the starting hoop. Players can only move forward and diagonally.

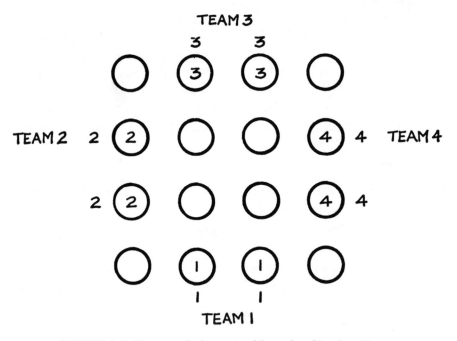

FIGURE 6-1. Hoop and player positions for Checker Hoops

Variations:

1. Increase the strategy by allowing each team to determine which player will move when it is that team's time to move.

2. Let the player who lands in a hoop with another player determine the open hoop to which that player must return.

3. Increase the number of hoops and let more students play at one time.

NONVERBAL UNSCRAMBLE

Object: To learn various methods of nonverbal communication and to encourage cooperation under difficult conditions.

Equipment: None.

Description:

Have teams of four to twelve and as many teams as are needed. Each person on each team is given a number. The players are positioned so they are not in numerical order. On a signal from the teacher, all the students shut their eyes and then line up in numerical order without verbal communication.

Variations:

1. Have one team go at a time so the other players can watch the fun.

2. Require the teams to make different shapes by the way they line up. To make it even more difficult, have them make various shapes while on the floor.

3. Give each of your students the name of an animal and have them line up according to the size of the animal. All participants keep their eyes open in this variation and they portray the animal they represent by moving like the animal.

4. Another variation would be to use the name of the animal to line up alphabetically.

GET IN SHAPE

Object: To develop physical fitness.

Equipment: Use available equipment.

Description:

Physical fitness activities can be effectively used with large classes. Try some of the following when faced with a large class.

1. Mass jog or walkathon. Add variety by using other forms of locomotion. The principles of interval training can be taught by alternating a strenuous activity such as skipping with a moderate activity of walking.

2. Circuit training. Make use of existing equipment and facilities either indoors or outdoors. Increase the number of stations as class numbers increase. Operate the stations on a timed basis so the class will keep moving.

3. Obstacle course. Children of all ages love an obstacle course. Adjust the difficulty of the obstacles to the ages and skills of the participants. Include going over, under, and around equipment, as well as skill obstacles such as being required to walk while straddling a rope representing a river.

4. Exercise trail. Develop an exercise trail on your school grounds. Have exercise stations at regular intervals along your trail. Your students can start at different points along the trail and proceed at their own pace by interspersing jogging and/or fast walking with exercise repetitions at the exercise stations.

5. Field Day. A field day type of activity is excellent for large classes. Field days must be carefully planned and organized thoroughly or they can be disastrous.

EXPLORER

Object: To provide movement excitement for younger children.

Equipment: None.

Description:

One child is designated as the explorer. All the other players have their own spots on the floor. The explorer asks, "Who wants to go exploring with me?" Those who do fall in behind the explorer who leads them around the gymnasium or a field area. When the explorer yells, "I found it" all the children run back to their places. The first child back is the explorer for the next game.

Variations:

1. The explorer can be required to find something that students have been studying about in another class and use this as a signal to return to their places.
2. The explorer can call out some form of locomotion which must then be used by all the players to return to their spots.
3. Animal names can be used and the students make the sound of that animal when running to their starting places.

STEAL THE BACON TUG OF WAR

Object: To pull the rope out of a circle.

Equipment: A strong rope approximately ten feet long.

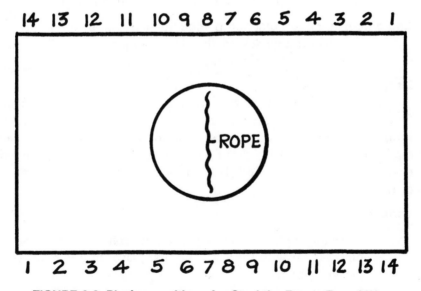

FIGURE 6-2. Playing positions for Steal the Bacon Tug of War

Description:

Divide the class into two teams and give each player a number. Place the rope in a circle in the middle of the floor. The teacher calls a number and the player on each team with that number runs to the rope and tries to pull the other player over the line for a team point. It is also a team point if the rope is pulled out of the circle before the opposing player can grab it.

Variations:

1. Call out several numbers each time.
2. Set up several circles with a rope in each one. Players can go to any circle. The element of strategy enters into this variation since a team can overload one circle and "hold" the other circles until help arrives. Players can move to other circles when they are successful in scoring a point. Losing players must go back to the sideline.

ENDURANCE ROPE

Object: To keep from being touched with a circling rope.

Equipment: One six-foot jump rope for each group of jumpers; painted circles on the floor; foam rubber ball or yarn ball tied to the jump rope for weight.

Description:
Students stand around the circles that are painted on the floor. One person stands in the center of the circle with the weighted jump rope and slowly starts to turn the rope so the ball follows the circle on the floor at a height of no more than one foot. The speed of the turning rope is varied. If the rope touches anyone, he is out of the game temporarily.

Variations:

1. Have a line of players ready to enter each circle. When one player is hit with the ball, the first player in line takes that player's place.
2. Keep all players jumping and see how few times members of a team are hit during a designated time period. It is best to have a member of each team turning the rope for his team.

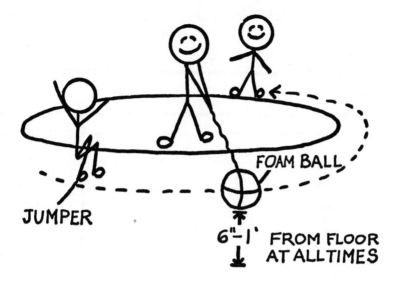

FIGURE 6-3. Set-up for Endurance Rope

SOCK THE BOX

Object: To hit a box with balls to drive it across the opponent's scoring zone.

Equipment: One to three boxes and as many balls as possible.

Description:

The boxes are placed an equal distance from two teams. Each team starts with an equal number of balls. When a signal is given, the teams begin firing at the box, trying to move it across their opponent's point line. One point is scored each time a team is successful. This can be played on a timed basis to determine the winner. With small children, the teacher keeps the balls out of the middle. Older children throw with enough speed to cause the balls to roll within reach of another player.

Variations:

1. Have four teams play by using a square formation.

2. With extremely large classes, rotate a new group of players into the game after every score or every two minutes.

3. Have easier or more difficult items for the players to "sock."

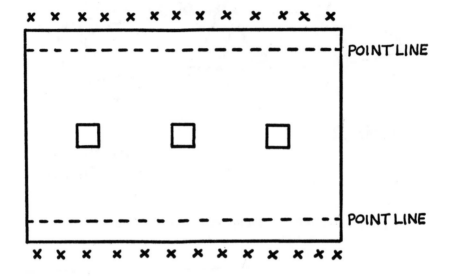

FIGURE 6-4.
Court positions for Sock the Box

FLOAT BALL

Object: To keep a beach ball in the air for the longest period of time.

Equipment: A beach ball for each group.

Description:
Form groups of ten to twelve students. Each group bats the ball in the air on a signal from the teacher. The winning team is the one that keeps the ball in the air the longest.

Variations:

1. Have the players play from a seated position or while on their knees.

2. Require the players to remain stationary when standing on their feet.

3. Use balloons instead of beach balls.

4. Vary the size of the circles or use formations other than a circle.

BLAST BALL

Object: To throw the foam rubber ball into a goal marked on the wall.

Equipment: Foam rubber ball and pinnies for one team.

Description:

This game can be played best in an area enclosed by four walls with minimum obstructions along the walls. The players sit on the floor with their feet out in front of them. They must remain in this position. They can slide to a different location on the floor when they do not have the ball. The game is started with a center drop between two players. Each team tries to score a goal by passing the ball to one of its players who is in position to throw the ball into the goal. The goal should be about four feet high and three feet wide and can be designated on the wall on each end of the floor with tape or paint. A neutral zone which is off-limits to all players should be designated in front of each goal in order to keep the emphasis on offensive play.

Variations:

1. Use a playground ball and require the players to propel the ball by kicking, throwing, rolling or punching.

2. A larger goal area can be designated.

GAME MODIFICATIONS

SUPER VOLLEYBALL

Object: To reinforce hand-eye coordination and develop teamwork skills.

Equipment: Two volleyball nets and standards; utility ball at least three feet in circumference.

Description:

The dimensions of the playing area for this game are at least two volleyball courts placed side by side. There can be anywhere from ten to thirty students on a side. A coin flip decides which side will hit the ball first. The ball may be hit with both hands either open or closed. There is no limit to the number of times a ball may be hit on one side of the net and each player can hit it as many times consecutively as desired.

In order to score a point, the ball has to strike the floor inbounds on the opponent's side. After each point has been scored, the ball is put into play by the side that was just scored on.

Variation:

Allow the players to catch, throw, and run with the ball on their side of the net.

CONE BALL

Object: To score more runs than the other three teams.

Equipment: Softball and bat; bases; three cones.

Description:

This game is played with four teams of six to ten players. Teams are numbered and bat in sequential order with all the members of a team batting before the teams rotate. The teacher pitches the ball to each batter who hits the ball and runs around the bases without stopping. When team one is batting, the other three teams are out in the field with one team playing third base and the left side of the field, another team playing second base and the middle of the field, and the last team playing first base and the right side of the field. Teams rotate from batting to first to second to third. The teams in the field must retrieve the batted ball and throw the ball around to each base. A cone is placed about five feet from each base. Each cone must be knocked down. If the batter reaches home before all three cones are down, one team point is scored. If the cones are knocked down first, no runs score.

Variations:

1. Require the fielders to move inside hoops.
2. Use a kickball instead of a softball and bat.

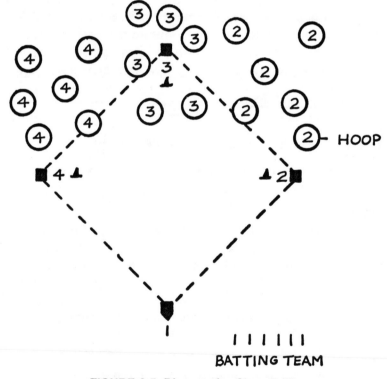

HOOP

BATTING TEAM

FIGURE 6-5. Diagram for Cone Ball

BACKBOARD CAGE BALL

Object: To score a team point by hitting the backboard with the cage ball.

Equipment: A large cage ball and pinnies for one team.

Description:
Fifty or more students can play this game on a small crosscourt basketball court. Players can be anywhere on the court. The game is started by tossing the ball in the air in the center of the floor. Students try to keep the ball in the air and advance it to their basket. A point is scored when the ball hits any part of the backboard. If the ball becomes deadlocked on the floor or against a wall, it is tossed up in the air to start play again.

Variations:

1. Have the players all sit on the floor and play for one-minute periods. The team that has the ball on its opponent's half of the court at the end of one minute receives one team point. The players can be anywhere in the playing area.

2. Require the players to use only their feet to move the ball.

B-BALL

Object: To learn the skills and rules of volleyball.

Equipment: A beachball for each game and a net (or rope to represent a net) for each game.

Description:
This is a good game for the lower grades and can also be used effectively for older students when you have a large class. The size of the court is determined by the ages and skills of the students. Badminton-size courts work out well. The students sit on the floor and play volleyball over a net that is three to six feet high. The game is started by someone in the front row throwing the ball over the net.

Variation:
Place a sheet over the rope so that the students will not be able to tell from which area the ball is coming. This variation can be used for any net game.

SKY BALL

Object: To score points by kicking the ball through the goal, throwing the ball through a hoop, or running or passing the ball across the endline.

Equipment: Soccer ball; four cones; two hoops with rope to attach them to the goal.

Description:

A field the size of a football or soccer field is best for this game. Twelve to thirty-six players can be on a team. Approximately twelve players from each team are on the field at one time. A fresh group of players is substituted for each team after each score and every three to five minutes. Action is continuous and players may play anywhere on the field.

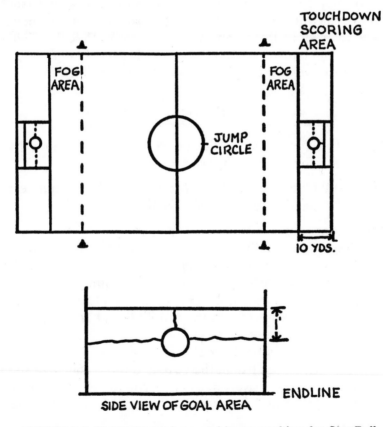

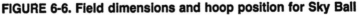

FIGURE 6-6. Field dimensions and hoop position for Sky Ball

A jump ball is used to begin the game and after each score. Players may kick the ball as in soccer, or convert it to an aerial ball so they can run with the ball or pass it to a teammate. An aerial ball is a ball that is caught in the air immediately after being kicked by the person catching the ball or by another player.

There are three ways to score in Sky Ball. A kick through the goal post counts one point. A touchdown by passing or running is worth two points. Three points are given for "hoopla" which is successfully throwing the ball through the hoop. In order to score a touchdown, a player must run through the "fog" area without being tagged, or receive a pass in the touchdown scoring area from a teammate who is not in the "fog" area. To score a "hoopla," the ball must be thrown from outside the "fog" area and a goal must also be kicked from outside the "fog" area.

A player who is tagged while carrying the ball must immediately drop the ball and play it as in soccer. If a foul (such as unnecessary roughness, or touching a ball that hasn't been converted to an air ball) is committed, a free throw to score a "hoopla" is given from outside the "fog" area. Balls going out of bounds are given to the opposing team for an unobstructed kick in.

EVERYTHING GOES

Object: To score a goal by kicking, throwing, or running the ball into the opponent's goal.

Equipment: One soccer ball and two goals, which should be about one-half the size of a regular soccer goal.

Description:

Players are distributed evenly throughout the playing area, with one person allowed to be a goalie. The game is started in the center of the field with a jump ball. After the jump ball, the teams attempt to work the ball to their opponent's goal area. The ball can be moved by kicking, throwing, or dribbling, but not by running with the ball.

One point is scored for throwing the ball in the goal, two points for kicking the ball in the goal, and three points for running the ball in the goal. Players must be within ten yards of the goal in order to run the ball into the goal. If a player is tagged in the goal

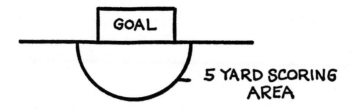

FIGURE 6-7. Goal area for Everything Goes

area while trying to run for a goal, the ball goes over to the other team.

Variations:

1. Vary the size of the goal according to the ages and skills of the players. Use cones if a goal is not available.
2. Require the teams to alternate kicking and throwing the ball when they move it up the field.

Index